Tax Guide 202

HOBBY BUSINESS VENTURES

by

Holmes F. Crouch
Tax Specialist

Published by

Allyear Tax Guides

**20484 Glen Brae Drive
Saratoga, CA 95070**

ISBN   0-944817-18-1

LCN 93-72404

Printed in U.S.A.

Series 200
Investors and Businesses

Tax Guide 202

HOBBY BUSINESS VENTURES

For other titles in print, see page 224.

The author: **Holmes F. Crouch**
For more about the author, see page 221.

PREFACE

If you are an inquiring-minded **taxpayer** looking for ideas, this book can be helpful to you. It is designed to be read — from cover to cover — in less than six hours. Or, you can skim read it in approximately 30 minutes.

Either way, you are treated to **tax knowledge** . . . *beyond the ordinary*. The "beyond" is that which you cannot find in official instructions, and that which is not imparted to you by computer programs.

Taxpayers have different levels of interest in a selected tax subject. For this reason, this book starts with introductory fundamentals and progresses through some rather complex situations. You can verify the progression by chapter and section in the table of contents. In the text, "applicable law" is quoted in pertinent part. Key interpretive phrases and key tax forms are emphasized. Real-life examples are given . . . in down-to-earth style.

This book has 12 chapters. This number provides depth without cross-subject rambling. Each chapter starts with a head summary of meaningful information.

To overcome the humdrum of ordinary tax jargon, informative diagrams and tables are placed strategically throughout the text. Most of the illustrations are true originals. By leafing through page by page, reading the summaries and section headings, and glancing at the diagrams and tables, you can get a good handle on the matters covered.

Effort has been made to update and incorporate all of the latest tax law changes that are significant to the title subject. However, "beyond the ordinary" does not encompass every conceivable variant of fact and law that might give rise to protracted dispute and litigation. Consequently, if a particular statement or paragraph is crucial to your own specific case, you are urged to seek professional counseling. Otherwise, the information presented is general and is designed for a broad range of reader interests.

The Author

INTRODUCTION

"Hobby business? What's that?" you ask.

It's a business venture that you engage in . . . on the side. It's a spare time business, so to speak. It's something you do in your off-duty moments which, someday, you hope, will blossom into the real thing. It's that dream that you have in the back of your mind that just won't go away. It keeps popping up year after year when your thoughts otherwise are in neutral.

Engaging in a hobby business implies that you are working full time, or essentially full time, in some other endeavor. You may be an executive in a large company, an employee in an established business, an independent professional (actor, doctor, attorney), or self-employed in a business of your own. In any event, your hobby business is not your primary source of income for livelihood. Your hobby business produces some income, but nowhere sufficient in amount to support your lifestyle.

The term "venture" implies that your hobby business activity may not endure long term. It is an interesting endeavor to try, to see if it works out. If it does not work out the way anticipated, the venture can be terminated. In its place, an alternative hobby business can be instituted.

Hobby businesses are those which develop as an outgrowth from your engagement in some sport, hobby, recreation, or travel activity. You entered one or more of these activities initially for the pure pleasure and enjoyment that you derived from them. As time and opportunities unfold, you see a chance to convert your contacts and expertise into some form of substantial business endeavor. Unfortunately, it is your initial entry motive that makes your business intentions therewith tax suspect.

The tax suspicion of a hobby business is cast in concrete in the Internal Revenue Code. The particular law on point is **Section 183**. It is titled: *Activities Not Engaged In For Profit*. This is a "stand-alone" section which the IRS falls back on when none of its other general disallowance rules apply. Section 1 8 3 presumptively disallows all business-type expenditures which exceed the income from your hobby-type business.

We are going to tell you a lot about Section 183, and how you can use it to *your* tax advantage. After all, if you invest money in a hobby business, and you indeed earn some income from it — however modest — you want all the tax deductions that you can legitimately claim. In particular, you want as deductions those expenditures which *exceed your income* from such activity.

To claim your excess-of-income hobby business expenses, you need to become familiar with the tax finepoints of the following Form 1040 schedules, namely:

Schedule C: Profit or Loss From Business

Schedule D: Capital Gains and Losses

Schedule E: Supplemental Income and Loss

Schedule F: Profit or Loss From Farming

Virtually any type of hobby business that you might conceive of with profit potential somewhere down the line will use one or more of these four 1040 schedules. The Form 1040, of course, is your own income tax return which you file annually, and to which you attach one or more of the above schedules.

Whether you launch a side business from your activity in a sport (such as golfing, swimming, hiking, racing), a hobby (such as train models, artistic works, antiques, stitchery), a recreational item (such as vacation cabin, yacht, airplane, off-road vehicle), or some travel trip (to China, Russia, Australia, South Africa) you'll need to know the many tax traps of Section 183. Realizing this, we'll devote separate chapters to its many interpretive aspects. We're also going to review (briefly) various Tax Court cases involving approximately **85** different types of hobby businesses. We want you to get the sense of the *judicial mind* — NOT that of the IRS — when approving/disapproving hobby business matters. With the various judicial rulings to guide you, you'll be in a much better position to stand up to the IRS when it scrutinizes — as it eventually will — your hobby business activities.

In a free enterprise system, every individual is entitled to "try his hand" at some new business venture . . . even if he derives some personal pleasure from it. If expenditures are made in good faith, one wants them to be tax deductible in full, whether they exceed the income derived or not. There is more to Tax Life USA than working full time to generate revenue solely to support Big Government.

CONTENTS

1

STATUTORY HURDLES

> By Their Nature — Sports, Hobbies, Travel, And Entertainment — Hobby Businesses Are More Tax Suspect Than Livelihood-Type Businesses. Various Tests And Hurdles Are Designed To Eliminate Those Without Economic Substance And Material Participation By The Owner(s). At Minimum, 100 to 500 Hours Or More Of Personal Time Each Year Are Required. Transactions Between Related Taxpayers And Closely-Held Entities Are Restricted, And AT-RISK Investment Rules Apply. The IRS Uses Discretionary CAD/263A Techniques To Postpone Your Otherwise Legitimate Deductions As Long As Possible.

Our goal in this book is to familiarize you with the special tax rules (and their nuances) for claiming full deductions with respect to your hobby business ventures. Before explaining these rules, however, we want to acquaint you with the various tax hurdles, tax theories, and tax tests that you first have to overcome. If you are going to engage in a business venture that is not your primary source of livelihood, you'll find many statutory and definitional obstacles in your path.

From "day one" of the income tax laws, non-livelihood businesses have always been tax suspect. They are treated as tax shelters rather than serious businesses. Because of their entrepreneurial aspects, they cannot be outlawed altogether. Some may truly blossom into bona fide ongoing businesses. Those that do blossom must pass various administrative and judicial tests designed strictly to limit or disallow the expenditures therewith.

For example, one of the first hurdles you must pass is the economic "performance" rule. Upon passing this test, you are subjected to the economic "substance" (sham transaction) rule. Then you must carefully structure your dealings with related taxpayers, or the use of recreational property, to be at "arm's length." And, as if this were not enough, you have to thread your way by the at-risk limitation rules, the material participation rules, and the CAD/263A discretion of the IRS. These matters are necessary prerequisites for carrying on an effective hobby business.

You want to go into your hobby business — or continue in it — with your eyes open. In this regard, do not try to be too, too tax clever in your entrepreneurial endeavors.

Economic Performance Test

It has been the practice for many years for persons in side businesses and tax shelters to wait until the last days of December to post their "books of account" for the year. They did this under the guise of year-end tax planning. There is nothing evil or illegal in doing so.

The idea was that, in December, if you wanted to reduce your reportable income for the year, you merely **postponed** depositing (for record purposes) selected income items. That is, even if you had payment checks in hand, you delayed accounting for the income until January of the following year.

Where expenditures were to be made, and there was a desire to accelerate deductions so as to reduce one's taxable income, the practice of **prepaying** for expenses arose. This meant that if one were intending to order, say, $10,000 worth of supplies in February, he would pay for them in December. This would — allegedly — permit one to claim the deduction in the December-ending year.

In other words, the year-end game plan was to postpone income and accelerate deductions. To a limited extent, this permitted one to manipulate his taxable income to his choosing.

The Internal Revenue Code treats these machinations as *distortions* of income. Tax distortions arise because of the "time value of money" . . . the theory goes. The IRS loses money based strictly on the time lapse between the reporting event and the actual performance event.

Year-end tax distortions violate the spirit of Section 446(b): Methods of Accounting. This section reads, in part, as—

If the method of accounting . . . used by the taxpayer . . . does not clearly reflect income, the computation of taxable income shall be made under such method as, in the opinion of the [IRS], does clearly reflect income.

Needless to say, giving the IRS power to recompute taxable income at will only encourages reverse distortion. The IRS grossly overcompensates. It sets up its own hypothetical "all events" tests to justify its assessing the maximum tax possible. Misuse of Section 446(b) by the IRS has led to much litigation.

To put an end to the reverse distortions by the IRS, Congress, in 1984, came up with the economic performance rule. It enacted Section 461(h)(2): ***Time When Economic Performance Occurs.*** The gist of this rule is that—

(A) *If the liability of the taxpayer arises out of—*
*(i) the providing of services to the taxpayer by another person, economic performance occurs **as such person provides** such services;*
*(ii) the providing of property to the taxpayer by another person, economic performance occurs **as the person provides** such property; or*
*(iii) the use of property by the taxpayer, economic performance occurs **as the taxpayer uses** such property.*
(B) *If the liability of the taxpayer requires the taxpayer to provide property or services, economic performance occurs **as the taxpayer provides** such property or services.* [Emphasis added.]

The idea underlying Section 461(h) is that one's entry of record (for tax purposes) must be made *as and when* each performance event actually takes place. That is, each item of income is reported, and each item of deduction is claimed, in that year in which the event reality took place. The term "event reality" means the legal rights and legal liabilities being performed on each side of an arm's-length transaction. No more juggling the books for best year-end tax benefits.

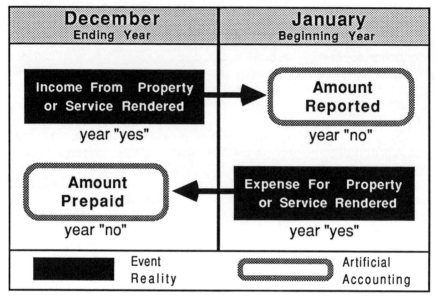

December Ending Year	January Beginning Year
Income From Property or Service Rendered year "yes" →	**Amount Reported** year "no"
Amount Prepaid year "no"	← **Expense For Property or Service Rendered** year "yes"
▇ Event Reality	▭ Artificial Accounting

Fig. 1.1 - Role of "Event Reality" In Tax Accounting

We portray the economic performance concept in Figure 1.1. The concept is basically that of event reality versus artificial accounting.

Habitually making your accounting entries only at the end of the year is a dead giveaway that your hobby venture is more tax motivated than business motivated. Proper business motivation is exemplified when your accounting chores are more or less regularly entered throughout the year. If you do so consistently, economic performance becomes self-regulating.

Time Lapse CAD Tools

The concept of economic performance for business-tax accounting is fine. But, unfortunately, the IRS carries the concept to its extreme. It uses its famous three tools — C, A, D — for deferring deduction event entries as long as possible. The three tools are Capitalization (C), Amortization (A), and Depreciation (D). Though these are established accounting principles, the IRS uses them to maximize revenue without regard to reality. Let us explain.

Capitalization. You buy a territorial franchise in a business, which protects you from like-kind competition as long as you hold the franchise. You pay all cash, say, $100,000. There is no question about the expenditure event and the contract you signed (it could have been a sports franchise). Do you get an immediate deduction for this?

No! Your $100,000 has to be capitalized. This means that your capital is "frozen in time" until you either sell the franchise or abandon it down the road somewhere. You acquired a capital asset. It has indefinite life and is not subject to wear and tear [IRC Secs. 1221, 1253(b)].

Amortization. Instead of buying a franchise outright, you spent money over several years investigating and creating your own hobby business territory. Wisely, you accumulated these expenses in a separate account. When they reached $30,000, say, you finally opened your business (or offered your services). When the income started in, you decided to write your investigative expenditures off as a tax deduction. Is this correct?

No! Your $30,000 has to be amortized. This means that you write the expenditures off ratably over the projected income stream of your start-up business. Amortization is a month-by-month allocation of creative-type expenses over a period of not less than 60 months [IRC Sec. 195(b)(1)].

Depreciation. You are an avid race-track fan and decide one day to buy your own race horse. You pay $50,000 for a 2-year-old thoroughbred. You hire a professional trainer, a professional jockey, and you invite accreditation track officials to oversee your qualification program. During off-training hours and weekends, however, you allow children, relatives, and friends to ride the horse and take care of it. Under special rules for race horse training (which we'll tell you about in Chapter 2), you start deducting the training expense on your tax return. Can you take any deduction for the purchase price of the horse itself?

Yes ... but! You have to depreciate the horse over its statutory class life. After all, the horse *is* subject to wear and tear, and to disease and death. If the horse is strictly for racing purposes, and you allow no personal use of it, you can depreciate the $50,000 over three years. But, since you allow personal use of it, the IRS would class it as "other than a race horse." In such case, you'd have to depreciate it over at least seven years or longer [IRC Sec. 168(e)(3)(A), (C)].

It is obvious — or should be — from the above that the IRS uses its CAD tools for one purpose only. It is to maximize the federal revenue. It does this by stretching out your otherwise legitimate deductions as long as possible. The IRS can be quite unreasonable and intransigent in these matters.

Related Taxpayer Transactions

A hobby business, by its very nature, attracts entrepreneurial arrangements between family members, close friends, business associates, and controlled entities (such as partnerships, trusts, and corporations). The close-knit arrangements evolve because a hobby business is unlikely to attract investors who are strangers. The intended venture tends to be speculative and risky. It is devoid of the regulatory protections of public offerings.

When there are close family and friends in a business setting, the monetary, property, and service transactions between them are tax suspect. This is because the competitive bargaining of adversarial give and take is missing. In its place, favors are exchanged, prearrangements are made, and tax shiftings occur. Income may be assigned arbitrarily to lower tax-rate participants, while deductions may be assigned to those participants having higher tax rates. Interest-free loans may be made, and the transfer of appreciated property at a loss may be contrived. The net result is a glaring mismatch of accounting events without regard for the economic performance rule.

All of this is a tax no-no. Section 267 of the IR Code especially forbids such activities. The full, official title of this section is: *Losses, Expenses, and Interest With Respect to Transactions Between Related Taxpayers*. This no-no section consists of approximately 2,000 mandatory words.

The gist of Section 267 is covered by its subsectional items, namely:

Subsec. 267(a)(1)	Deductions for losses disallowed.
" " (2)	Matching (required) of deduction and payee income for expenses and interest.
Subsec. 267(c)(1)	Rules for constructive ownership of stock.
Subsec. 267(d)(1)	Amount of gain where losses previously disallowed.
Subsec. 267(f)(1)	Rules applicable to controlled groups.
" " (2)	Deferral (rather than denial) of loss from sale or exchange between members.
" " (3)	Certain foreign currency losses.

The whole idea of Section 267 is that related taxpayers — be they individuals or entities — cannot pass through to each other income, losses, interest, or expenses without there being some *direct matching* on each side of the transactional slate. The matching must occur within a 2-1/2-month period after the close of each taxable year. This 2-1/2-month grace period is to allow for different methods of accounting (cash vs. accrual) between individuals (on a calendar year) and entities (on a fiscal year).

The intent of Section 267 is to dampen the voluntary switching around of tax benefits between related participants who are separate taxpayers. Subsection 267(b) defines related taxpayers as those listed in Figure 1.2. On the persons and entities so listed, Section 267 imposes an added accounting burden which is not imposed on those who are not related.

Closely-Held Entities

Somewhat akin to the related taxpayer entities in Figure 1.2 are "closely-held" entities. A closely-held entity is a partnership, trust, or corporation (usually of the S-type) in which five or fewer participants hold more than 50% of the ownership interest in the entity. These five participants need not be and often are not related in any Section 267 way. Their common interest is close economic control of the entity. Even if there were 10 or 100 other participants with ownership interest in the entity, the five "close ones" pretty well run the show. This economic closeness provides a golden opportunity for conducting hobby business ventures.

Let's postulate an example based on true life cases.

Through word-of-mouth, the close principals learned that an upstart movie company had produced a master film for which it had no money for its promotion and sale. The film was titled: "Iguassu Falls: Up and Over." It cost $150,000 for its production. No established film producer was interested in promoting it.

> *Editorial Note*: Iguassu Falls is one of the three great natural waterfalls of the world. It is 2.5 miles wide and drops 210 feet. It is located in South America between Argentina and Brazil. Very few U.S. persons have ever visited it.

The five close principals hired a business consulting firm to appraise the U.S. market potential of the Iguassu film. The consulting firm prepared a 5-year projection of income from the

	Related Taxpayers as Defined by IRC Sec. 267(b)	
	Relationship	Comments
1	Members of a family	Brothers, sisters, spouse, parents, ancestors, descendants, etc.
2	Individual & corporation	Where individual owns more than 50% value of the stock
3	Two corporations	Members of controlled group with same over 50% owners
4	Grantor & fiduciary	Of same trust; Grantor conveys money: Fiduciary manages it
5	Two fiduciaries	If same person is grantor of both trusts; Same beneficiaries
6	Fiduciary & beneficiary	Of same trust; Beneficiary receives money that fiduciary manages
7	Fiduciary/beneficiary	Of different trusts; Where same person is grantor of both
8	Fiduciary & corporation	Where over 50% of the stock is owned by the trust or by its grantor
9	Individual & charity	Where charitable organization is controlled by family of individual
10	Corporation & partnership	Where same persons own over 50% interest in both entities
11	S corporation & S corporation	Where same persons own over 50% of stock in both entities
12	S corporation & C corporation	Where same persons own over 50% of stock in both entities

Fig. 1.2 - List of Related Taxpayers for Suspect Transactions

sales and rentals of the film to be $3,000,000 or, on average, about $600,000 per year. By using the "income capitalization" method, the film's appraised market value was set at $1,000,000.

Following the appraisal report, the close principals offered the film maker $50,000 cash plus 20% royalties on all sales and rentals. The offer was accepted, and each of the five principals put up $10,000 cash. They formed an S-type corporation (Iguassu Distributors) and began marketing the Iguassu film. [An S-type corporation consists of 35 or fewer U.S. shareholders with pass-through accounting features similar to a partnership.]

On the S-corporation's books, the master film was listed with a "cost or other basis" at $1,000,000, depreciable over five years. This produced a depreciation deduction pass-through of $40,000 per year to each of the five close principals. [$40,000 x 5 yrs = $200,000; $200,000 x 5 principals = $1,000,000 cost or other basis.]

Mind you, each close principal put up only $10,000 of his own money. Yet each was able to take a depreciation deduction of $40,000 each year for five years. Do you see anything wrong here? It was all legal and, tax technically, correct.

Be introduced now to a special rule directed at hobby business venturers and tax shelter participants.

At-Risk Limitation Rule

You know in your own heart that investing $10,000 in a business venture and taking a $40,000 tax deduction each year for five years (total: $200,000) is not right. And it isn't. This is the gist of Section 465 of the tax code.

Section 465 is titled: *Deduction Limited to Amount at Risk*. Subsection (a) thereof reads in essential part as—

*In the case of an individual . . . engaged in an activity to which this section applies, any loss from such activity for the taxable year shall be allowed **only to the extent of the aggregate amount** with respect to which the taxpayer is at risk . . . for such activity at the close of the taxable year.* [Emphasis added.]

Section 465 applies to those activities involving motion picture films, video tapes, farming, leasing tangible personal property, oil and gas resources, and geothermal deposits [IRC Sec. 465(c)(1)].

Thus, in the Iguassu Falls illustration above, the amount at risk (per individual) at the close of the first taxable year is $10,000. This becomes the amount deductible: NOT the $40,000 depreciation deduction postulated.

What about the second and subsequent taxable years?

Answer: There are no further deductions unless the *aggregate amount* exceeds $10,000. The term "aggregate amount" is the initial investment **plus** the net investment income from the activity each year. The net investment income is gross income less expenses less depreciation. If the net investment income each year is insufficient, the full theoretical depreciation may never be deducted.

HOBBY BUSINESS VENTURES

The amounts considered at risk are defined more expressly in subsection (b) of Section 465. This subsection reads in essential part—

A taxpayer shall be considered at risk for an activity with respect to—
   (A) the amount of money and the adjusted basis of other property contributed by the taxpayer to the activity, and
   (B) amounts borrowed with respect to such activity . . . to the extent that [the taxpayer] *. . . is personally liable for the repayment of such amounts, or has pledged property . . . as security for such borrowed amount (to the extent of the net fair market value of the taxpayer's interest in such property).*

In a sense, the close participants in the above Iguassu Falls illustration borrowed money from the original owners of the master film. They "borrowed" $100,000. The original owners paid $150,000 for production of the film. They received $50,000 in cash plus a lucrative royalty contract. As part of that royalty contract, $100,000 could be construed as borrowed money. That is, the $100,000 was "secured" by the master film itself. On this point, however, subsection 465(b)(2) specifically says—

No property shall be taken into account as security [for borrowed money] *if such property is directly or indirectly financed by indebtedness which is secured by property* [used in the activity itself].

Thus, unless business venture participants borrow money from a commercial lending institution (for which they are personally liable for repayment), or pledge property which they own outside of the business venture itself, they are not at risk for such other amounts.

All forms of indirect borrowings are classed as *nonrecourse financing*. They are expressly excluded from at-risk computations [Sec. 465(b)(4)]. We want you to be fully aware of this fact. To assist your awareness in this regard, we present Figure 1.3.

Importance of "Material Participation"

There is still another important deduction limitation rule for you. This is Section 469 which is titled: *Passive Activity Losses and Credits Limited.*

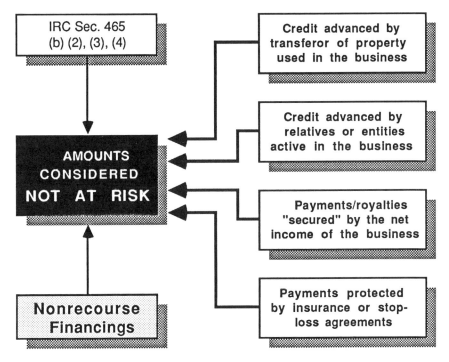

Fig. 1.3 - Financings Eliminated by At-Risk Rules

The gist of this rule is that if you are a participant in a passive activity, the maximum tax deduction that you are allowed is limited to the net income from such activity. Section 469(c) defines a passive activity as—

Any activity—
(A) which involves the conduct of any trade or business, and
(B) in which the taxpayer does not materially participate.

Where Section 465 (At-Risk Limitations) targets only certain activities (movie films, farming, oil and gas, etc.), Section 469 encompasses **any** trade or business in which the owners thereof do not materially participate. This raises the logical question: What is meant by "material participation?"
Subsection 469(h) defines the term as—

> *A taxpayer shall be treated as materially participating in an activity **only** if the taxpayer is involved in the operations of the activity on a basis which is—*
> *(A) **regular**,*
> *(B) **continuous**, and*
> *(C) **substantial**.* [Emphasis added.]

This is a rather qualitative definition. Are there any quantitative standards that one can use? Yes, Regulation 1.469-5T(a) sets forth seven objective tests that can be used. Some of these are quantitative tests based on hours of participation during the tax year. For example, material participation is satisfied if one—

* Participates in the activity for more than 500 hours during the tax year.
* Participates in the activity for more than 100 hours during the year, and his participation is not less than the participation of any other person.
* Participates in a manner which constitutes substantially all of the participation in the activity of all individuals (including nonowners) for the tax year.

There are no specific recordkeeping requirements for proving the extent of your participation. Any reasonable evidence may be used, such as: appointment books, calendars, narrative summaries, absence of paid managers, and time cards on paid persons serving less than 100 hours. At the very minimum, you must be able to show at least 100 hours of participation . . . and, preferably, more than 500 hours.

If you qualify as a material participant in your hobby business, Section 469 does not apply. This means that, except for the hobby loss rule of Section 183 (to be discussed in Chapter 2), your net loss from the business can be used to offset other sources of your tax accountable income. If your hobby business is not of the Section 465 type (movie films, farming, oil and gas, etc.), then Section 465 does not apply either.

Be Mindful of Section 263A

Section 263A is one of the most confusing and complex tax laws ever. It is officially titled: *Capitalization and Inclusion in Inventory Costs of Certain Expenses*. It is the phrase "certain expenses" where all the confusion and complexity arise. This phrase is a blatant attempt by the IRS to force the capitalization of otherwise current expenditures which, even remotely, can be "allocable" to a business's regular inventory held for sale (rental or distribution) to customers. This is the IRS's previously described CAD routine in another form. We certainly want you to be mindful of this section.

Section 263A consists of over 3,600 words. It is statutized in nine principal subsections, each subsection having multiple sub-subsections of its own.

The gist of Section 263A is set forth upfront in subsection (a): **Nondeductibility of certain direct and indirect costs.** Then the first sub-subsection thereunder reads (in part)—

In general — *In the case of any property to which this section applies, any allocable costs* [direct and indirect]—
   (A)   which is inventory in the hands of the taxpayer, shall be included in inventory costs, and
   (B)   in the case of any other property, shall be capitalized.

The lead-in phrase "In general" is your tip-off that there are some exceptions.

The property to which Section 263A applies consists of the following:

263A(b)(1)   — *Real or tangible personal property **produced by the taxpayer**.*
263A(b)(2)   — *Real or personal property . . . which is **acquired by the taxpayer for resale**.*
               [Emphasis added.]

Thus, the type of "applicable property" envisioned in Section 263A pretty well covers most items likely to be involved in hobby business ventures.

To explain and interpret Section 263A, the IRS has promulgated some 85 pages of regulations. These regulatory pages comprise **more than 65,000 words!** This is insane tax policy. Our conclusion is that Section 263A is a tribute to the weakness of Congress and the power and greed of the IRS. The only practical salvation is that the rules are so complicated that the IRS's personnel themselves do not know how to interpret and apply them correctly.

Fortuitously, there are some exceptions to the applicable property rules. Of these, one is particularly important to hobby businesses. It is sub-subsection **263A(b)(2)(B)**; this section provides an exception where the gross receipts from property acquired for resale are less than $10,000,000 ($10 million) for any taxable year. Its official title reads: EXCEPTION FOR TAXPAYER WITH GROSS RECEIPTS OF $10,000,000 OR LESS.

We doubt that many hobby business owners will attain 10 million dollars in gross receipts annually. Should your hobby business reach this point, why continue it as a hobby? Why not make it a full-time business?

Sham Transactions: Beware!

A sham transaction is a disingenuous arrangement between a taxpayer (hobby business venturer) and one or more entities over which he has significant economic control. The usual entities involved are: (1) tax shelters, (2) foreign partnerships, (3) charitable trusts, (4) dummy corporations, (5) personal holding companies, (6) controlled groups, and others. These entities — though perfectly legal on paper — are shell-game *fronts* for disguising those financial transactions which are **not** at arm's length. The term "arm's length" refers to the give-and-take of adversarial and above-board competitive interests. As we'll point out shortly, any tax attributes resulting from a sham transaction can be ignored . . . totally.

To give you the flavor of what constitutes a sham transaction, here are four different Tax Court cases which have been ruled on:

Case 1 — *R. LiButti*, TC Memo 1985-314

The taxpayer set up a corporation in the name of his niece, to which he transferred his race horse and other business assets. Shortly thereafter, the racehorse died. The corporation collected the insurance proceeds. The Court ruled that the corporation was controlled by the taxpayer and served as a front for this and other tax evasion ploys.

Case 2 — *E. LaFargue*, TC Memo 1985-630

An attorney and several of his clients set up a complicated series of partnerships. They allegedly conducted business through these partnerships, thereby claiming interest deductions, amortization of a lease, management fee expenses, depreciation on buildings and cattle, and investment tax credits. The Court ruled that the arrangements lacked economic substance and were mere shams created for the tax benefits to be gleaned.

Case 3 — *C. E. Brimm*, TC Memo 1988-16

The taxpayer set up a tax-exempt charitable trust: "The Blessed Institute of Mercenary Missionaries." Separately, he operated a business providing engineering services to various aerospace firms. The income from this business was transferred to his blessed trust, from which he withdrew the money for personal living. No money went to any charitable cause. The Court ruled that the transfer was a sham involving paper transactions that had no substance.

Case 4 — *M. D. Fielding*, TC Memo 1992-553

The taxpayer and four investor friends formed a limited partnership purportedly to engage in oil and gas drilling. They paid a geologist to report on the feasibility of the venture, and to estimate the cost for drilling and developing 5 wells (1 well for each partner). The wells were never drilled, yet the partners took a 4-to-1 writeoff for the intangible drilling costs based on nonrecourse loans which never materialized. The Court ruled that the transactions were without substance, and denied all deductions that were taken.

Whenever there is suspicion of transactions without economic substance, the IRS has the statutory authority to **disallow all** tax benefits in connection therewith. This authority is found in Section 482: *Allocation of Income and Deductions Among Taxpayers.* The purpose of this authority is—

. . . to prevent evasion of taxes or clearly to reflect income of any . . . directly or indirectly controlled . . . organizations, trades, or businesses.

Our premise is that, if you are going to engage in a hobby business, do so in an entirely above-board manner. The best way to do this is to avoid creating sham-type entities which you and your co-investors control. Unless you absolutely have to have other people's money and participation, we see no point in creating some separate entity apart from yourself. By using your own Form 1040 Schedules C, D, E, and F, you can taxwise accomplish many of the same features of partnerships, trusts, and corporations. We'll have more to say on these 1040 schedules in later chapters.

Accuracy-Related Penalties

We hesitate to mention anything about tax penalties at this time. Yet, we must do so. These are risks which arise when the expense deductions you claim on your return cause you to pay a lower tax than the IRS figures you should pay. Tax penalty risks apply to all businesses, of course, but hobby businesses are far more vulnerable. All too hastily, the IRS will slap on the 20% accuracy-related penalty. This is an automatic add-on assessment for the slightest inaccuracies in your Form 1040 reportings. [IRC Sec. 6662(a)]

The most common assertion of the IRS is that of "negligence or disregard." Section 6662(c) defines these terms as—

[negligence is] *any failure to make a reasonable attempt to comply with the provisions of* [the Internal Revenue Code], *and the term "disregard" includes any careless, reckless, or intentional disregard.*

In the case of gross valuation misstatements, the 20% penalty can be increased to 40% [Sec. 6662(h)(1)]. In the case of sham transactions described previously, the IRS can impose the fraud penalty. This is a 75% penalty assessed against that portion of the underpayment which is attributable to fraud, as judged solely by the IRS [Sec. 6663(a)].

We are not trying to intimidate you with penalties the way the IRS does. We just want you to be aware that the IRS is "penalty happy." It treats all penalties as an arbitrary means for raising tax revenues without raising tax rates. The IRS can be — and often is — quite unreasonable and intransigent on these matters. All of which means that you must go out of your way to exercise due diligence when claiming hobby-business-loss deductions.

Due Diligence Summary

Because of the introductory importance of this chapter, we want to summarize and highlight the key points made. The idea is to go into your hobby business venture with the intention that your bona fide expenses and deductions will be allowed. The best way to do

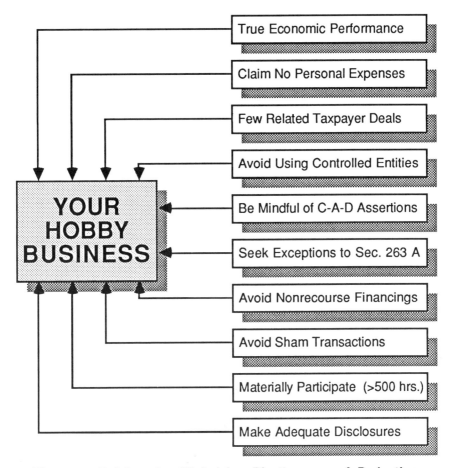

Fig. 1.4 - Pointers for Minimizing Disallowance of Deductions

this is to disregard most of the friendly tax tips that you may have received from others. Each hobby business is a separate tax target of its own. The IRS is not swayed by what other hobby venturers have done, may do, or do not do. The facts and circumstances in each case are addressed separately.

Proceed in your business with the expectation that you'll be tax-challenged at every step of the way. In reality, this will not happen. The IRS bureaucracy has its own inertia and blindspots to contend with. Nevertheless, proceed as though you were fully aware of the tax laws affecting your business, and as though you were ready to be challenged on any of them.

Abide by the concept of "economic performance" (event reality) before claiming your deductions. Make sure that your transactions all have economic substance (not shams), and that you do not engage in "creative" nonrecourse financings. Put your own money or property on the line. Take the direct risks yourself. If you lose, and there is minimal evidence of personal pleasure or personal living from the venture, at least your net losses will be recognized in one form or another.

Even when you exercise maximum due diligence in your hobby business affairs, the IRS will still attempt to force you to defer your deductions over the longest period of time possible. This is because of its adversarial policies of C-A-D (Capitalization, Amortization, Depreciation) . . . and Section 263A (capitalization and inclusion in inventory). When confronted with its CAD/263A assertions, stand your ground and appeal. Know the tax law on which you rely, and review relevant Tax Court decisions therewith. The IRS is not always right; it often overreaches its interpretive discretion.

By their very nature — activities involving sports, hobbies, travel, and recreation — hobby businesses are always tax suspect. Minimize these suspicions by going out of your way to avoid transactions between related persons and closely-controlled entities. You can do this by either yourself, spouse, or hirees *materially participating* in the affairs of the business. This participation does not require full time, though anything less than 100 hours per year will be deemed "immaterial." The safe harbor for participation is 500 hours (60 days) or more for the year.

To deflect those inevitable tax penalties that will be assessed against you, make sure that all material facts are adequately disclosed on your return, or in a statement attached to it. Where valuation amounts are required, engage a professional appraiser to provide realistic computations thereon. In all other respects, make every effort to show that you have not been careless, reckless, or negligent in your tax reportings.

For future reference when highlighting your due diligence efforts, we present Figure 1.4. This diagram will be useful in later chapters, as a kind of quick summary of those preparatory matters that are essential to any tax-successful hobby business. Intentionally omitted from Figure 1.4 is any reference to the *hobby loss rule* itself. This special rule is espoused in Section 183 of the tax code. This is what the next chapter is all about.

2

SECTION 183 OVERVIEW

Section 183 Is Generally Known As The "Hobby Loss Rule." Its Central Thesis Is A PRESUMPTION That If You Do Not Make A Profit In 3 Out Of 5 Consecutive Years, You Are In A NOT-FOR-PROFIT ACTIVITY. The Stigma Is That Your Net Losses Are Disallowed. You May be Allowed Certain Expenses . . . But Only To the Extent Of Your Income. If Your Activity Resembles That Of Section 162 Or Section 212 (Livelihood Businesses), You Have A Better Than Even Chance Of Your LOSSES Being Allowed. Particularly So, If You Hold To Section 6501(a) Which Limits The IRS's Assessment Authority To 3 Years For Additional Tax.

In Chapter 1, we introduced you to approximately eight separate sections of the Internal Revenue Code having some bearing on your business endeavors. Although we framed these sections as though they were directed at hobby businesses, in reality they are directed at any and all business forms where the expense deductions exceed the actual income from such ventures. Those sections are what we call the "preliminary qualifying barricades" for justifying *any deductions* on your return . . . whether individual or entity.

In this chapter, we want to focus strictly on Section 183 of the IR Code. This section specifically targets hobby businesses. Although the term "hobby" is nowhere used in the statutory wording of Section 183, its target is pretty clear from its official heading. That heading is: *Activities Not Engaged in for Profit*. From this heading alone, the clear implication is that Section 183 targets for special attack all forms of businesses that are **not** livelihood sustaining for the owner(s) thereof.

Section 183 attempts to straddle the requirements of Section 162 (personal-service intensive businesses) and Section 212 (income-property intensive businesses). Both Section 162 businesses and Section 212 businesses are treated as livelihood-seeking businesses. As such, they are not hindered by the implications of personal pleasure and enjoyment that hobby businesses entail.

When you are through this chapter, we want you to be comfortable and confident in your knowledge of Section 183. We want you to know this section forward and backward, and all the subsections in between. This intimate knowledge will enable you to claim your legitimate deductions in full, as you incur them.

In General: A Presumption

There is a basic and underlying tax thesis to Section 183. Embodied between each of the words of its heading (Activities Not Engaged in for Profit) is a *statutory presumption*. The presumption is that if you do not make a net profit from your business in any three out of five consecutive years, you are some kind of flake trying to beat the government out of its revenue.

We want to stress that the thesis of Section 183 is a **presumption** only. It is not some new law of economics. It is not a dictate of Congress, as the IRS would have you believe. It is not a law that rules out business recessions, business disasters, product liabilities, customer lawsuits, or plain old-fashioned bad luck in your otherwise genuine endeavors. It is a presumption for the convenience of "protecting the revenue" of government. This is the true and basic thrust of Section 183.

The not-for-profit presumption is set forth in reverse, in subsection 183(d): *Presumption*. The entire first sentence thereof reads—

If the gross income derived from an activity for 3 or more of the taxable years in the period of 5 consecutive taxable years which ends with the taxable year, exceeds the deductions attributable to such activity (determined without regard to whether or not such activity is engaged in for profit), then, unless the [IRS] establishes to the contrary, such activity shall be presumed for purposes of [the IR Code] *for such taxable year to be an activity engaged in for profit.* [Emphasis added.]

This citation is all one sentence: 80 words. It is back-handed ... and rather heavy-handed, too. It has some tricky nuances, such as "attributable to" and others.

If your income exceeds your deductions in three out of five consecutive years, and the reverse is true (deductions exceed income) in two of the same five years, it is *presumed* that you are in business to make a profit. The corollary presumption is that you are in that business for livelihood reasons, or at least for contributing towards your livelihood. Therefore, your two years of losses may be allowed.

The not-for-profit aspect of Section 183(d) derives from its reverse connotations The reverse connotation is that if you do not make a net profit in any three out of five consecutive years, there are other reasons than livelihood for your being in that business. Therefore, your excess deductions which produce the net loss may not be allowed.

Spot the Catch Phrases

Of the 80 words in the first sentence of subsection 183(d), there are five ominous "catch phrases." These are what the IRS relies on to twist the law against you. If you know where the catch phrases are, you can put your own spin on them before the IRS comes on the scene.

The five catch phrases as they sequentially appear in 183(d) are:

1. ... *income derived from an activity,*
2. ... *which ends with the taxable year,*
3. ... *deductions attributable to such activity,*
4. ... *unless the* [IRS] *establishes,*
5. ... *for purposes of* [the IR Code].

To comprehend the chicanery of this tax law, you have to consider phrases 1 and 3 together. In phrase 1, the emphasis is on income (from **an activity**); in phrase 3, it is on deductions (attributable to **such activity**). Concentrate for the moment on the words "an activity" and "such activity." Could not the IRS deliberately partition your hobby business into two *separate* activities: an income activity and a deduction activity?

Do you recall some of our comments in Chapter 1 about the IRS being authorized to allocate income and deductions in any manner that it sees fit? The ostensible reason for this allocation power is to clearly reflect income, maximize revenue, and prevent tax evasion. But, more often than not, the IRS reallocates your income and deductions just for the sport of it.

Example: Recall our Iguassu Falls travel film in Chapter 1. Suppose, from the master film itself, you selected certain frames and made enlarged still photographs. They were gorgeous scenes of nature: breathtaking waterfalls, wild flowers, dangling trees, jutting boulders, and so on. These scenic photographs sold like wildfire. They generated substantial income with little cost on your part. Simultaneously, the movie rentals produced meager income, while your deductible costs were substantial. Nevertheless, overall you generated a modest net income for the taxable year.

In a situation like this, what do you suppose the IRS would do?

Answer: The IRS would "determine" — that's an official dogma — that you have **two** separate activities. Activity 1 would be the scenic photo business; activity 2 would be the film rental business. Activity 1 produces substantial net profit from which substantial tax revenues would flow. Activity 2 produces substantial net loss, but the loss would be disallowed [Subsection 183(a)]. Now do you see the chicanery in conversely written tax laws?

The IRS can go so far as to partition your hobby business into two, three, four, or more separate activities — whatever produces the maximum revenue pain. Yes, it can. Yes, it will. Yes, it does. Talk to any long-term business venturer who has been through the hobby activity partitioning mill: audits, appeals, Tax Courts . . . and more appeals.

The partitioning of a hobby business for maximum tax effect is an IRS practice of longstanding. Using our Iguassu Falls example, we emphasize this partitioning in Figure 2.1. The IRS picks apart every separable function that it can, and treats each as a separate activity. To countermand the IRS, you have to show a clear and convincing connection — **an inseparability** — between the different facets of your business.

The "Taxable Year" Phrase

Catch phrase 2 above draws attention to the year *which ends* with the taxable year. You are probably saying to yourself: "What

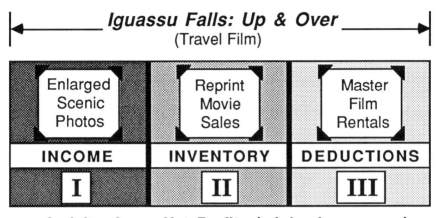

Activity I - **Net Profit** (minimal expenses)

Activity II - **Capitalization** (minimal sales)

Activity III - **Net Loss** (disallowed)

Fig. 2.1 - How IRS Partitions Hobby Ventures for Maximum Tax

possibly could be the catch here? The phrase means what it says." Does it?

Bear in mind that, in Section 183, we are dealing with a period of five consecutive tax years. Only one of the five may be the taxable year. The term "taxable" means some amount of additional tax over and above that which is shown on the original return; that is, some *assessed amount* or deficiency. Which one year in the five years are we talking about? It is whichever year the IRS picks.

Suppose years 1, 2, and 3 were profit years, and years 4 and 5 were loss years. The IRS picks year 5 to examine your business records. Unless there were glaring understatements of income and overclaiming of deductions, you would satisfy the for-profit presumption of Section 183.

But, suppose the IRS picked year 6, which also happened to be a loss year. Your five consecutive years would be: years 2 and 3 (the profit years) and years 4, 5, and 6 (the loss years). Since you have three loss years in a row, your motivations are presumed not-for-profit. As a result, your deductions in excess of income for the three loss years would be disallowed.

Suppose you have a net profit in year 7. What would be the effect then?

Your five consecutive years are: year 3 (profit), years 4, 5, and 6 (losses), and year 7 (profit). If year 7 is picked by the IRS, can it arbitrarily disallow all three loss years 4, 5, and 6? Don't answer too quickly. There's a *statute of limitations* that we want to tell you about . . . right now.

Section 6501(a): ***Limitations on Assessment of Tax***, limits the IRS's assessment authority to three years after a return is filed. Specifically, subsection 6501(a) says, in part—

> *The amount of any tax imposed by* [the IRS] *shall be assessed* **within 3 years** *after the return was filed . . . and no proceeding in court without assessment for the collection of such tax shall be begun after the expiration of such period.* [Emphasis added.]

Now, back to answering the year 7 question above. In practical terms, if the IRS picked year 7 for examination, it would be at least year 8, and possibly year 9, before your return would be examined. Normally, it takes about 18 months after a return is filed for you to be officially notified which year has been selected for examination. The net result is that, even though you may have three or more loss years in a five consecutive-year period, not all of those loss years are within the IRS's assessment grasp.

The "Unless IRS Establishes" Phrase

Catch phrase 4 above raises another concern over the authoritarian power of the IRS. The actual phrase in subsection 183(d) is—

> *unless the Secretary establishes to the contrary.*

The "Secretary" is the Secretary of Treasury, of which the IRS is part. So, what is this catch phrase getting at?

Two things, actually. One, even if you met the three-out-of-five-years-for-profit presumption test, the IRS can override the presumption. It can assert, unilaterally, that you were **not** engaged in that hobby business for profit. It can assert, for example, that you intentionally doctored your records to show a profit in the three qualifying years. It may allege that you included phantom income and that you did not claim all allocable deductions. These assertions imply that your activity was a sham.

Secondly, if the IRS alleges that your taxable-year activity was a sham, you are guilty of filing a false return. A false return invokes the first of nine exceptions to the 3-year limitation on assessments. On this point, subsection 6501(c)(1): *Exceptions; False Return*, reads—

> *In the case of a false or fraudulent return with the intent to evade tax, the tax may be assessed, or a proceeding in court for collection of such tax may be begun without assessment, at any time.* [Emphasis added.]

By claiming that you filed one false hobby business return, the IRS can open up and examine all of your returns, back to year 1 of your hobby business. All it needs to allege is one plausible fact to support its position. You then have to disprove the IRS.

What appears to be an innocent tax phrase to the casual reader can unleash some rather draconian assertions by the IRS.

The Circumvention Phrase

The most innocent-appearing phrase of all in Section 183(d) is phrase 5 listed above. This phrase is: *for purposes of* [the IR Code]. The actual statutory wording is—

> *for purposes of this chapter.*

The term "this chapter" refers to Subchapter B of the IR Code: Computation of Taxable Income.

Many federal tax laws use this particular phrase (for purposes of this *section, paragraph, chapter, title, subpart,* etc.) over and over again. You have to wonder why this is done, not just in Section 183(d), but throughout the entire tax code. You probably have no inkling of the real reason.

Did it ever occur to you that the IRS acts, at times, *extraconstitutionally*: outside of our constitutional precepts?

The IRS can come on the scene, literally tear your business apart, reallocate income and deductions, disallow any loss benefits, accuse you of filing a false return . . . ALL WITHOUT ANY PROOF on its part. Does this not strike you as being violative of your constitutional rights: "innocent until proven guilty"?

While at times the IRS's behavior may strike you as being violative of your rights, it is NOT. When administering federal tax laws, the IRS enjoys the theory called: *presumption of correctness*. That is, the IRS is presumed correct because it is interpreting the laws for income tax purposes only. If it goes beyond these laws, it may well have violated your civil and constitutional rights. But these rights are not at issue here. We are addressing Section 183 which addresses the taxable income aspects of hobby businesses only.

In other words, catch phrase 5 is a protective clause for the IRS. It protects the IRS against any allegation you may make that its reallocation and disallowances are violative of your basic rights. It is in this sense that phrase 5 *circumvents* the U.S. Constitution in its entirety.

Second Sentence in 183(d)

Thus far, we've covered only 80 words of the entire Section 183. These words comprise one sentence only — the first sentence — of subsection 183(d): Presumption. There is also a second sentence. It consists of 34 words and reads in full as—

> *In the case of an activity which consists in major part of the breeding, training, showing, or racing of horses, the preceding sentence shall be applied by substituting "2" for "3" and "7" for "5."*

In this second sentence, we have an entirely different time period for the for-profit presumption. Instead of three profit years out of five, there need be only two out of seven. Of particular note, however, this two-out-of-seven presumption applies only to *horses*: the breeding, training, showing, or racing thereof. In other words, if your hobby business activity involves horses in some manner, you can have as many as five loss years (in a consecutive period of seven years) and the losses (if otherwise bona fide) could be allowed.

How come a more favorable time period applies to horses, and not to other animals such as pedigree dogs, orangutans, endangered elephants, etc.? Isn't this a case of "unequal treatment" under law?

If we were not dealing in tax law, there would be a case for unequal treatment. But, under catch phrase 5 above (for purposes of the IR Code), Congress and the IRS can ignore the unequal treatment arguments. Furthermore, the U.S. Supreme Court has ruled on various occasions that Congress can enact tax laws that treat different *classes* of taxpayers differently. As long as there is equal treatment within a given class, not all hobby businesses have to be tax treated equally. So much for theory.

You know in your heart what happened. The horse owners association of America lobbied Congress for its advantage. Apparently, the lobbyists argued that the *breeding, training, showing, or racing* of horses is a highstakes, infrequent profit business that requires more for-profit preparatory time than other businesses involving animals or nonanimals. But couldn't the same argument be made for alpacas, giraffes, or giant pandas? Yes, but there are probably more horse lobbyists in Washington than there are panda lobbyists.

At this point now, we have three separate time frames for profit consideration. Timeframe 1 is the regular 3-year statute of limitations for assessing additional tax. Timeframe 2 is the 5-year period for all hobby businesses except horses. And timeframe 3 is the 7-year period for horses. We display all three of these in Figure 2.2. This depiction helps you to better visualize the relative risks that you might be willing to take, even though you may incur losses in two, three, or more consecutive or intermittent years. We'll come back to Figure 2.2 later.

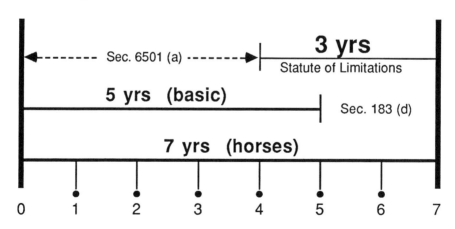

Fig. 2.2 - Time Periods for Hobby Profit Considerations

General Disallowance: 183(a)

Except for favoring horses (five loss years out of seven), Section 183 is structured purposely to disallow losses (deductions exceeding income) from hobby businesses. The general rule to this effect is set forth in its subsection (a). This subsection is one entire sentence of its own. It reads in full as—

*In the case of an activity engaged in by an individual or an S corporation, if such activity is not engaged in for profit, **no deduction attributable to such activity shall be allowed** under this chapter* [of the IR Code] *except as provided in this section.* [Emphasis added.]

The language is pretty concise. No deduction shall be allowed if the activity is deemed not for profit. Actually, this means all deductions . . . except as provided elsewhere in Section 183. We already know of one particular exception: the three-out-of-five (and two-out-of-seven) presumption of subsection 183(d). There are other quasi-exceptions that we'll get to shortly.

In the meantime, note the phrase: *an individual or an S corporation.* Why do you suppose an S corporation is singled out? One reason is to make a distinction that C-type corporations (unlimited shareholders) are not affected by the hobby loss rule. Why do this?

Simply because, in a C corporation, any net losses stay in the corporation itself. Said losses cannot be passed through to the individual shareholders. The beauty of hobby losses, if allowed, is that they can be used by individuals to offset other forms of positive income on their tax returns. Consequently, why would you engage in a hobby business in C corporate form, where there is no chance that you could benefit on your personal returns from several years of allowable losses?

In contrast, an S corporation is a small business or *pass-through* entity, much like that of a partnership or trust. Certain deductible losses and credits can be passed through to individual participants, in proportion to their ownership interests.

Also, note the phrase: *deduction attributable to such activity.* As an individual, you can deduct your allowable hobby losses on Schedules C, D, E, and F (of Form 1040) where it is pretty clear to the IRS where your deductions are claimed. In the case of a pass-through entity (partnership, trust, or S corporation), the "attributable" aspect of your deduction has to be examined at the entity level. You, as an influential participant, may have taken one attributable amount, whereas the IRS may come up with a different version. It **will** come up with a different version if your entity is closely controlled or involves related taxpayers.

Applicable Activity Defined: 183(c)

Earlier we said that the word "hobby" is nowhere mentioned in Section 183. This is true. What is mentioned is the phrase: *activity not engaged in for profit.* By deductive reasoning, this phrase certainly includes hobby businesses. It also includes tax shelters, related-party transactions, charitable efforts, recreational activities, and the like. These are quite clearly not-for-profit endeavors. Our use of the word "hobby" is a simpler collective term meaning the same thing.

Subsection 183(c) defines the phrase: "activity not engaged in for profit" as—

*any activity **other than** one with respect to which deductions are allowable for the taxable year under **section 162** or under . . . section 212.* [Emphasis added.]

We need to clarify for you what Sections 162 and 212 are.

Section 162 is titled: ***Trade or Business Expenses.*** Its general rule, subsection 162(a), reads in introductory part—

*There **shall be allowed** as a deduction all the ordinary and necessary expenses paid or incurred during the taxable year in **carrying on** any trade or business . . . .* [Emphasis added.]

The idea here is that if you are carrying on a trade or business on a regular, continuous, and substantial basis [material participation: Sec 469(h)(1)], your "ordinary and necessary" deductions *shall be allowed.* Carrying on such a business implies that you are seeking a profit for livelihood purposes. If you are not engaged in such a business, you must be in a not-for-profit activity (hobby?).

Section 212, on the other hand, is titled: ***Expenses for Production of Income.*** There are no subsections to Section 212. It reads in full as—

In the case of an individual, there shall be allowed as a deduction all the ordinary and necessary expenses paid or incurred during the taxable year—
   (1) for the production or collection of income;
   (2) for the management, conservation, or maintenance of property held for the production of income; or
   (3) in connection with the determination, collection, or refund of any tax.

Again, you see the phrase "ordinary and necessary" expenses . . . for the production of income, or for management of property (held for the production of income). If you are not holding property for the production of income, or are not engaged in producing income in some other regular and ongoing manner, 183(c) says that you are in a not-for-profit activity (hobby?).

It is quite evident that there is a message of opportunity in subsection 183(c). The activity defined therein seems to take on a "sandwich role" between Sections 162 and 212. We try to depict this role in Figure 2.3. Our hunch is that you could structure your hobby business to resemble either a Section 162 activity or a Section 212 activity, or some combination of both. If you did so, you would have a better than even chance of overcoming the presumption of 183(d), and of circumventing the disallowances of 183(a). Regulations to Section 162 and 212 prescribe that loss years (when deductions exceed income) are indeed allowable, regardless of frequency or consecutiveness.

Deductions Allowable: 183(b)

Figure 2.3 is intended to beam a subliminal message to you. Not so subliminal is the message in subsection 183(b): *Deductions Allowable*. Its focus part is—

In the case of an activity not engaged in for profit . . ., there shall be allowed—
   (1) the deductions which would be allowable under [the IR Code] *. . . without regard to whether or not such activity is engaged in for profit, and*
   (2) a deduction equal to the amount of the deductions which would be allowable . . . if such activity were engaged in for profit, but only to the extent that the gross income derived

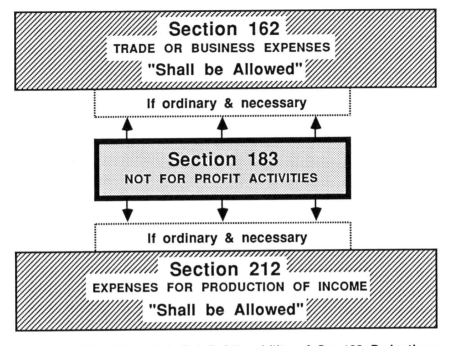

Fig. 2.3 - The "Sandwich Rule" Allowability of Sec.183 Deductions

from such activity . . . exceeds the deductions allowable by reason of paragraph (1).

What are these two paragraphs really saying?

Paragraph (1) says that, regardless of the general disallowance rule of 183(a), if your expenses qualify under other sections of the tax code, they are allowable, whether you are in a hobby business or not. Typical examples are property taxes, investment interest expenses, tax audit expenses, casualty losses, capital losses, etc.

Paragraph (2) says that, after deducting the paragraph (1) expenses from the gross income (if any) of your hobby business, other bona fide expenses are allowable **but only to the extent** of the income remaining. In other words, if you derive any income from the business, you can always write off your expenses to the extent of the income derived. This means that you have no net profit . . . and no net loss. The bottom line is zero: a *tax wash*.

But we expect you to do better than this. You want the net loss writeoffs: not just a neutral bottom line. If you qualify under the

183(d) presumption, you could at least be allowed two or three loss years in each presumption cycle. The allowable losses can be used to offset other positive income sources you may have.

Forego the 183(e) Election

Subsection 183(e) titled: *Special Rule; Election*, makes a rather tantalizing offer. This subsection consists of four paragraphs totaling about 320 words. The gist of paragraphs (1) and (3) is that you can opt to postpone any examination (audit) of your hobby business returns until the 4th taxable year (6th in the case of horses) in the presumption period. You can elect this option by filing a special tax form. The special form must be filed within three years after the due date of the return for the first year you engaged in the hobby activity.

The election is made by completing **Form 5213**: *Election to Postpone Determination as to Whether the Presumption That an Activity is Engaged in For Profit Applies.* (This is the official heading on the form.) The form requires that you describe the activity in some detail. You can even file the form within 60 days after the IRS notifies you that it proposes to examine your return(s) for your hobby loss deductions.

The gist of paragraph (2) is that if you file Form 5213, the presumption provided by 183(d) shall apply, if, indeed, your income exceeded your deductions for the minimum profit years. In other words, the IRS will agree not to examine your return until after the 5th-year (or 7th) presumption period has expired. Does this sound like a good deal? Before answering, you should be aware of paragraph (4) of 183(e). You may want to forego the election.

Paragraph (4) of 183(e) is titled: *Time for Assessing Deficiency Attributable to Activity.* It reads in key part as—

> *If a taxpayer makes an election under paragraph (1) . . . the statutory period for the assessment of any deficiency attributable to such activity* **shall not expire before** *the expiration of 2 years after the* [due] *date . . . for filing the return of tax . . . for* **the last taxable year** *in the period of 5 taxable years (or 7 taxable years) to which the election relates.* [Emphasis added.]

Is it clear to you what subsection 183(e) says?

By filing Form 5213, you **waive** the normal 3-year statute of limitations for assessing additional tax. That is, you automatically extend the statute to two years *after* the 5th (7th) year in the presumption period This means that if the IRS asserts a deficiency in *any* of the presumption years it can assess other deficiencies back to year 1. To drive this point home, we present Figure 2.4. This depiction is a revisit of Figure 2.2 with the 2-year assessment extension tacked on.

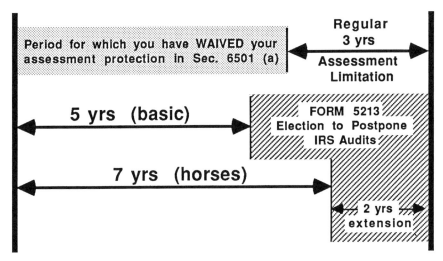

Fig. 2.4 - Impact of Form 5213 on Assessment of Deficiencies

We recommend against the subsection 183(e) election. If you file the election, it is tantamount to a guarantee of examination of your returns at the end of the 5th (7th) presumption year. You have then waived away your normal 3-year protection against assessments for additional tax. We think it is better to take your chances among the 115,000,000 (115 million) tax returns that the IRS has to "routinely process" each year. If you don't file the election, and some return of yours is selected for examination, the maximum assessment reach-back is three years. Why would you voluntarily want to give the IRS 5- or 7-year reach-back authority?

An Overall Perspective

Section 61(a) of the tax code defines your gross income as—

*any income **from whatever source derived,** including (but not limited to) the following items:* [Emphasis added.]

[some 16 items as listed on page 1 of your Form 1040]

Here, the term "income" also includes *loss.* This inclusion is automatically understood in any tax accounting situation. The possibility of loss is always part of the income-generating process. And, from the emphasized phrase above, the includible income/loss arises from "whatever source derived." Would not hobby business losses (if bona fide) be properly includible in your gross income on Form 1040?

Yes, certainly.

Furthermore, Regulation 1.162-1(a): ***Business Expenses; General***, concludes that—

*The **full amount** of the allowable deductions for ordinary and necessary expenses in carrying on a business **is deductible, even though such expenses exceed** the gross income derived during the taxable year from such business.* [Emphasis added.]

While this regulation is directed at livelihood-type trades and businesses, the concept is valid for any income-seeking endeavor.

Our point is that bona fide hobby business losses can be advantageous to you, when computing your taxable income. Trying to negate this advantage is what Section 183 is all about.

3

EXAMPLE COURT RULINGS

The Federal System Of Tribunals For Reviewing IRS's Disallowances Consists Of: (a) The Claims Court, (b) District Courts, And (c) The Tax Court. Since 1970, Many Case Rulings On Section 183 Losses Have Been Founded Upon Two "Tests," Namely: A - PROFIT MOTIVE, And B - ECONOMIC SUBSTANCE. Failing These Two Tests Means That Your Activity Is A Sham. No Deductions Are Allowed . . . And Penalties Are Imposed. The One Area More Prone To Deduction Success Involves Highly Specialized Activities. These Require Financial And Management Decisions Which Are INDEPENDENT Of Tax Consequences.

Entrepreneurship — free enterprise — is a deeply engrained political/social/economic philosophy in the United States. Most true businesses are started with the idea of making money — profit — somewhere along the line. Whether the business activity does or not is another matter. Yet in spirit, the profit motive is somewhere in the back of the mind of that individual who starts and carries on a business-like endeavor.

Where the profit motive is lacking, the endeavor becomes what Section 183 classifies as a not-for-profit activity. This classification severely limits the deduction writeoffs. Where economic substance also is lacking, there are no deduction writeoffs and penalties are assessed.

How is it determined whether an activity is engaged in for profit or not, or whether there is economic substance involved? How can the IRS "reach into the mind" of the entrepreneur to determine these matters?

The answer is that the IRS does **not** reach into a taxpayer's mind in any objective way. It makes an off-the-cuff call, disallows all related deductions, and leaves it up to each activity owner — YOU — to move the matter into court for judicial review and ruling.

Approximately 10 to 20 Section 183 cases reach the courts each year. Less than half of these go to full trial. This has been going on steadily since about 1970. As a result, there is now a substantial body of rulings on which we can rely for judging what is best to do and not to do, for hobby business success. We will review some of these cases for you . . . after a brief introduction to our judicial process.

Federal Court System

There are three entry-level tribunals for hearing tax matters. There is the U.S. Claims Court, the U.S. District Court, and the U.S. Tax Court. All three are courts of *original jurisdiction*. This means that all prior papers and documents submitted to, and adversarial stances by, the IRS are disregarded. The trial starts anew (de novo) whereby the judge hears "both sides" to the extent that he or she deems relevant.

Of the three courts so named, each is an embodiment of the three separate branches of government: Executive, Judicial, and Legislative. The Claims Court has jurisdiction over all monetary claims against the federal government, such as damage awards, entitlements, tax refunds, etc. The District Court has jurisdiction over all federal questions, such as rights issues (criminal, civil, states), actions against government officials, tax refunds, etc. The Tax Court has jurisdiction over all tax deficiencies asserted by the IRS that arise from its administration of the Internal Revenue Code. The general organizational arrangement of these three courts is presented in Figure 3.1.

The Claims Court and the District Court deal only with tax refunds: NOT tax deficiencies. There's a difference. The difference is that in order to proceed into the Claims Court or into the District Court, you have to first *pay* the tax and penalty, seek a refund of it through the IRS, and, when disallowed, then petition the Claims Court or District Court for its refund. Whereas the Claims Court handles tax refund suits of $10,000 or less, the

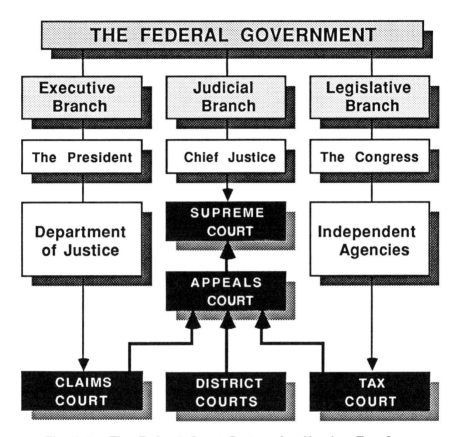

Fig. 3.1 - The Federal Court System for Hearing Tax Cases

District Court handles refund suits over $10,000 (including all penalties).

The Tax Court is unique in that paying the tax is not required in order to get a hearing on your case. The only requirement is that the IRS must issue you a formal Notice of Deficiency, alleging the amount of tax due and penalty. Within 90 days, you have to formally petition the Tax Court for a *redetermination* of that deficiency.

Each court has its own separate rules of procedures and practices. All require that the tax item at issue be IRS disallowed and that formal "pleading papers" be filed by the taxpayer and by the IRS. With the exception of fraud, tax evasion, and criminal allegations by the IRS, the **burden of proof** in any of the court proceedings is directly **on the taxpayer**. This is the very reason why the IRS can be so cavalier about its disallowance of Section 183 issues. Because tax issues are involved, rather than rights issues, all three courts tend to rule in favor of the IRS so as to "protect the revenue" of government.

A judicial ruling by any of the three courts can be appealed to that Circuit Court of Appeals having jurisdiction over a designated geographic area.

> *Editorial Note*: The courts of appeals (CA) are located in the following cities: CA-1 Boston, CA-2 New York, CA-3 Philadelphia, CA-4 Richmond, CA-5 New Orleans, CA-6 Cincinnati, CA-7 Chicago, CA-8 St Louis; CA-9 San Francisco, CA-10 Denver, and CA-11 Atlanta.

Rarely — very rarely — are tax issues ever heard by the U.S. Supreme Court. The basic reason for this is that tax matters are viewed by the High Court as citizen *duty* issues: not rights issues. Every citizen and resident of the U.S. has a duty to pay taxes, as applicable. His/her basic constitutional rights are not involved. Because Congress enacted the tax laws for revenue purposes, the High Court is reluctant to interfere with this aspect of the "separation of power." As a consequence, any adverse ruling to a taxpayer by an entry-level court is entitled to only **one** review by a higher court, namely: the applicable Circuit Court of Appeals.

Congressional Intent Sought

When a lower court accepts a tax case for hearing, its first duty is to characterize the intent that Congress had in mind, when it enacted or amended the particular tax law at issue. That is, the court looks for the *intent phrase* in the enabling legislation.

In the case of Section 183: Activities Not Engaged in for Profit, the pre-1969 intent phrase was "reasonable expectation of profit." This phrase led to much subjective controversy. Whose "expectation" is to be judged? That of the taxpayer himself, or that of an external "reasonable person"? Is it a matter of playing a long shot if the potential rewards were great? Or, is the activity not for profit solely because a reasonable person would regard the chance of success as small?

In 1969, Congress abolished the "reasonable expectation" intent phrase and replaced it with the *engaged in for profit* phrase. For your recollection on this point, Section 183(a) rereads in part—

> *In the case of an activity . . . not engaged in for profit, no deduction attributable to such activity shall be allowed . . . .*

Here we see the phrase **engaged in** as being more discernible through objective, rather than subjective, analysis.

In the Senate Finance Committee Report on the 1969 amendment (P.L. 91-172), the underlying intent was stated as—

> Although a reasonable expectation of profit is not to be required, the facts and circumstances (without regard to the taxpayer's subjective intent) would have to indicate that the taxpayer entered the activity, or continued the activity, with the objective of making a profit. Thus, a taxpayer who engaged in an activity in which there was a small chance of a large profit, such as a person who invested in a wildcat oil well or an inventor, could qualify under this test even though the expectation of profit might be considered unreasonable.

In view of this stated Congressional intent, any judicial interpretation of Section 183 calls for some objective standard. The standard must be external to the taxpayer-petitioner. That is, the trier of fact — the trial judge — must determine whether the petitioner before the court entered into the activity with an honest objective of making an economic profit (as distinguished from a tax profit). In reaching his/her conclusion, a judge could ask himself/herself: Would a reasonable person conduct himself as the taxpayer has done (with respect to this activity) if his honest objective was to make a profit? Would a reasonable person play a long shot if the rewards are great enough?

The Judicial Mind

In a broad general sense, most federal judges tend to be impatient with taxpayers. They seem to think that every tax dispute is a frivolous matter that should not even be before his/her court. It is as though some judges have a mindset that every taxpayer is bellyaching because: "Who likes to pay taxes?"

There are some cases, however, where the judges take tax matters more seriously. They try to rationalize their rulings based on as many objective and diverse facts as they can glean from the proceedings. When such cases arise, you can get a feeling for the judicial mind at work. One such case relative to our discussion is that of *J. L. Rose* [CA-6, 89-1 USTC 9191, 868 F2d 851]. This was a 1989 District Court ruling that was upheld on appeal to the U.S. Court of Appeals 6th Circuit (CA-6).

The *Rose* case was that of a taxpayer who purchased reproduction masters of Picasso originals. He was going to put them on display, and sell them or rent them as opportunities arose. He purchased the masters at a price vastly in excess of their market value. He financed the purchase price largely by a nonrecourse note that was secured by the income from the masters themselves. The actual income derived was nil. Yet, the taxpayer wrote off his entire purchase price as a business loss. This kind of effort is called: *art publishing*.

The judge in this case took note of numerous facts presented — and unpresented — at trial. Among these facts was that the taxpayer had no prior knowledge of the fine art field. He made the purchase without seeking any expert advice. He didn't even question or compare the purchase price with other similar paintings in the art world. Although he claimed that he had hoped to make a profit, he was indifferent as to whether he did or not. He admitted that he was more persuaded by the tax advantages promoted by the seller than by any professionally appraised value. He undertook no significant retail or mail-order marketing effort.

To the court's way of thinking, there seemed to be no reasonable expectation of the taxpayer ever making a profit. The product was way overvalued at time of its acquisition. There was no marketing effort undertaken. No effort whatever was made to collect on the nonrecourse note. Other than a small down payment for a large tax writeoff, there was just no substance to the whole affair. In this case, the court ruled clearly against the taxpayer.

This case is instructional because it illustrates the lengths that some judges will go to unearth objective facts, even when such facts are often self-evident on the surface. A conscientious judge tries to reach beyond the self-serving statements of a taxpayer.

Prologue to Reasoned Rulings

In the *Rose* case, the trial judge came up with two specific tests for determining whether an activity is engaged in for profit. These objective tests are— A: profit motive, and B: economic substance

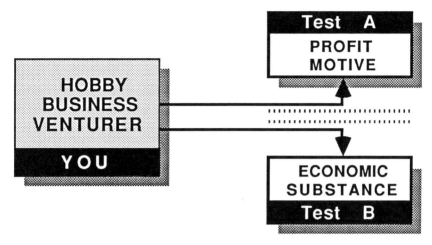

Fig. 3.2 - Key Tests for Surviving Sec.183 Disallowances

(as depicted in Figure 3.2). These two tests are fundamental to other rulings on Section 183 issues.

For example, suppose there was a situation where the taxpayer failed Test A (profit motive), but passed Test B (economic substance). What would be the result?

Answer: the deductions arising from the activity would be allowable to the extent of the gross income of the activity. This is the more typical hobby loss situation. The expenditures are actual, the debts (if any) are real, and the assets are purchased for their real value. But the facts lead to the conclusion that the taxpayer never expected or intended to make a profit.

Suppose the situation is such that the activity as a whole was engaged in for profit (Test A passing), but that certain aspects do not have economic substance (Test B so-so). What would be the result?

The deductions would have to be allocated between those aspects of the activity which lacked, and which had, economic substance. The deductions attributable to those aspects which lacked economic substance would be disallowed. The other deductions would be allowed, even though they produced a net loss. After all, there was profit motive.

If *all aspects* of the purported activity are without economic substance (Test B failure), what is the result?

The activity is a sham. No deductions whatsoever are allowable, regardless of any alleged profit motive. Section 183 does not even enter the picture. There is no investment, no indebtedness, and no expense. It is unnecessary to ask if the activity was engaged in for profit, because there is no activity. In addition, certain penalties — such as gross negligence and fraud — would be assessed.

Where an activity is overwhelmingly motivated by the prospect of tax losses, and there is indeed some out-of-pocket expenditures, some courts have held that the actual expenditures cannot be said to lack economic substance. However, the courts seem to be split over this point: some allow the expenditures; some don't. It is clear, though, that the profit motive is lacking.

Test A Failure Types

There are approximately 85 different types of hobby activities that have been judicially ruled on. These span the gamut of antiques, vintage autos, charter boats, coal leases, computer activities, health clubs, cattle breeding, parasailing, safaris, tennis, golf, travel agencies, treasure hunting, video games, mining ventures, cosmetic sales, music promotion, yachts, etc., etc. There are well over 500 Section 183 cases involved. The vast majority of those rulings adverse to the taxpayer were those where the profit motive was deemed lacking.

Once a judge decides that a genuine profit motive is lacking (Test A failure), he cites one *gist fact* to this extent, then rapidly concludes the case. To illustrate some of the gist facts stated in published rulings, we present the following Tax Court examples:

- *Private aircraft*

  Taxpayers (owning their own private aircraft) used the aircraft for sales demonstrations and flight instructions to their friends. The court held that the activities . . . *were in the nature of hobbies connected with plane ownership*, and therefore not for profit.

  — *J.F. Lemler*, 41 TCM 364, TC Memo 1980-507
  — *R.E. Akers*, 42 TCM 1548, TC Memo 1981-627
  — *L.W. Mueller*, 50 TCM 914, TC Memo 1985-450

- *Cosmetics, crafts, & gems*

  Taxpayers sold cosmetics, crafts, vitamins, gemstones, log cabin kits out of their homes, while having other full-time jobs. The court ruled that the activities . . . *were not carried out in a businesslike manner; no formal inventory or sales records were kept.*

  — *H.M. Goldstein*, 52 TCM 9, TC Memo 1986-339
  — *D.T. Ferrell, Jr.*, 53 TCM 209, TC Memo 1987-102
  — *J.F. Jackson, Jr.*, 61 TCM 2806, TC Memo 1991-250

- *Cattle breeding & farming*

  Taxpayers were highly-paid professionals who bought land, cattle, grape vines, chinchillas, and other assets to conduct breeding, farming, and ranching operations. The court ruled that said activities lacked the profit motive because the taxpayers . . . *did not have any prior experience* (on point), and that the land was purchased *primarily for pleasure instead of farming.*

  — *H. Mager*, 47 TCM 1651, TC Memo 1984-211
  — *T.E. Gerres*, 52 TCM 1119, TC Memo 1986-573
  — *R.L. Hawkins*, 54 TCM 1529, TC Memo 1988-17

- *Auto & motorcycle racing*

  ☐ *G.B. Zimmerman*, 35 TCM 559, TC Memo 1976-123
    — entered 13 motorcycle races on weekends during the year and never won a prize. No expenses deductible because no income earned.

  ☐ *L.E. Likes*, 61 TCM 3012, TC Memo 1991-286
    — did not engage in off-road pickup truck racing for profit reasons because of . . . *his lack of effort to recruit sponsors*, which was virtually *the only way to make money in off-road racing.*

HOBBY BUSINESS VENTURES

☐ *J.C. Dunkel*, 62 TCM 208, TC Memo 1991-336
— competed in a cross-country racing event for vintage automobiles and won a small prize. The court ruled that . . . *his interest in competing in this event was purely recreational.*

Certain Rulings Favorable

Not all hobby/sports/recreational-sounding activities are deemed lacking in profit motive. If conscientious effort is made in pursuit of the activity, and there is true economic substance involved, many court rulings have favored the taxpayer. We'll cite just three of these rulings to illustrate the extent of substance involved.

Take the case of *H.C. Plunkett*, 47 TCM 1439, TC Memo 1984-70. The taxpayer engaged in 4-wheel drive mud-racing and truck-pulling activities simultaneously. The court partitioned the activities into two separate categories, namely: (a) mud racing, and (b) truck pulling (pulling mud-racing vehicles out of the mud). The court held that the mud-racing competition had no potential for profit because the total possible winnings would have been significantly less than the expenses of competition.

As to the truck-pulling activity, however, the court allowed all of Plunkett's expenses, including losses. He carried on this activity in a workmanlike manner, and he was nationally ranked. He converted some of his mud-racing vehicles into truck-pulling vehicles without the assurance that he would be able to compete. The truck-pulling was honest and objective; his mud-racing was just incidental recreation.

Next take the case of *P. Dwyer*, 61 TCM 2187, TC Memo 1991-123. The taxpayer engaged in car racing for himself while helping to launch a racing career for his son. The court discounted the car racing for Dwyer himself because, as an attorney, he had sufficient income to incur large losses on his own behalf.

As to his son, however, the court ruled that Dwyer sponsoring his son's racing career was profit motivated. He investigated a major racing circuit before allowing his son to join. He consulted with racing experts and he and his son attended a high performance racing school. He discussed with his own accountant the accounting, financial, and tax aspects of the car racing business. He even set up a separate bank account for his racing business enterprise. His son showed real potential for earning winnings.

In the case of *D.K. Hatch*, 57 TCM 280, TC Memo 1989-202, the court ruled that the taxpayer had the requisite profit objective when operating a cattle breeding ranch. The Hatches (Mr. & Mrs.) carried on their activities in a businesslike manner, tried to minimize costs, and made a sincere effort to maintain adequate business records. They spent many hours working on the ranch doing chores (cleaning stalls, shoveling manure) that are not normally associated with pleasure. Furthermore, the taxpayers did not have the financial means to easily suffer their losses.

Many Horse Cases

In a period of 12 years — 1979 to 1991— there were some 80 cases heard involving the breeding, training, showing, and racing of horses. Bear in mind that these 80 cases represent just one of the 85 types of hobby businesses mentioned earlier. Horse-related activities comprise the most common single activity that the IRS goes after with a vengeance. That's why there were some 80 cases that went to trial. At least five times this many were disallowed by the IRS that never went to trial.

Of the 80 hobby horse cases, 50 were held not to be profit motivated. This left 30 cases where the profit motive was upheld. This is a favorable ruling of 3/8 or approximately 40%. As a Section 183 activity, this is probably the highest percentage of approval of any hobby business class.

The elements for approval when operating a horse-related activity are operating in a businesslike manner, and keeping good books and records. This was the essence of *D.R. Myrick*, 60 TCM 166, TC Memo 1990-368. Although the Myricks had no particular expertise in running a boarding stable or in training horses, they both had been raised on a ranch and had a great deal of experience in the care of horses. They expended extensive time and effort in carrying on the activity, keeping records of the vet visits and training sessions, and seldom actually rode the horses themselves. They showed losses in each of their years of operation, but the losses were decreasing.

In a similar case where losses were sustained year after year, the IRS tried to treat the breeding and racing activities as two separate operations, and required each to pass separately the profit motive test [*S.J. Trafficante*, 60 TCM 110, TC Memo 1900-353]. The trial court overruled the IRS. It recognized that breeding and racing were one overall activity. It understood — whereas the IRS did not —

that the breeding value of a horse increased if it was a good racehorse and produced offspring that fared well on the race track. Accordingly, the court held that Trafficante had an actual and honest objective of making a profit, thereby entitling him to claim *full deductions for the losses.* Trafficante simply did not have a knack for turning a quick profit in this or any other business endeavor.

In another case, *S. Thompson*, DC Conn, 90-1 USTC 50,043, the IRS tried to appeal a jury verdict that a horse breeding activity was conducted for profit. The IRS tried to show that the buying of land for the horse breeding operation was a separate investment activity of its own. The court refused to set aside the jury's verdict by holding that the land was nothing other than a necessary asset for the use and construction of facilities for the breeding and training of horses. The land had no other "higher use" potential.

Tax Court Misruling

Courts themselves sometimes make mistakes. Some judges get carried away with their power, and jump to hasty conclusions. They give short shrift to those cases which they perceive to be shams, especially if the IRS cajoles them enough.

In *J.R. Bryant*, CA-6, 91-1 USTC 50,157, 928 F2d 745, the Court of Appeals, 6th Circuit held that the Tax Court had erred in holding that a gold mining operation was a sham, and that it lacked economic substance. The Appeals Court noted that the gold mine was a bona fide operation; it just hadn't recovered much gold-bearing ore. Mining equipment was purchased and ore tailings were dug. Thus, obviously, the venture was not a sham.

The Tax Court came to its sham conclusion by using hindsight: the classic IRS tactic. It analyzed the financial merits of the mine by addressing whether Bryant had made a wise investment. It should have addressed first whether there was a bona fide investment, and next whether there was a profit motive. The Appeals Court instructed the Tax Court to take another look at *all* the facts and circumstances. It directed the Tax Court to keep in mind that a small chance of making a large profit could support a profit motive.

Upon remand, the Tax Court concluded that Bryant, who was the primary instigator, primary investor, and primary overseer, was appropriately profit motivated. However, his co-investors, who took on a purely passive role, were not so motivated. They were buying tax deductions rather than expectation of earning a genuine profit.

Mining operations — whether for coal, gold, gravel, oil, gas, geothermal deposits, etc. — bring into play various other sections of the tax code besides Section 183. If the venture is otherwise profit motivated, there are deductions for such expenditures as exploration, intangible drilling, development, depletion, and so on.

Buying Tax Benefits

Investing in a venture for tax reasons — that is, buying tax benefits — is not the same as investing for profit reasons. Nor is it the same as carrying on a business with economic substance in mind. When the amount of purported writeoffs in the first year exceeds the actual investment itself, we have what is classed as a *tax motivated* transaction. The true motivating factor arises from the tax benefits derived: NOT from the eventual livelihood aspects of the enterprise. As a result, said transactions are not tax recognized.

Tax motivation — in contrast to profit motivation — blinds one to the economic realities at hand. An exemplary case on point is that of *J.P. Meyers*, U.S. Claims Court: 55-88T, 9-17-92. The venture was promoted as "Gold for Tax Dollars" by the International Monetary Exchange (IME), a Panamanian corporation. The offering literature "promised" a $4 tax writeoff for each $1 invested. An investor was to deposit in cash one-fourth of the amount of the tax deduction he desired.

For the case cited, taxpayer Meyers alleged that he invested $100,000 in IME for a mineral lease consisting of 250,000 cubic feet of auriferous (gold bearing) gravel in Panama. The acquisition cost of this mineral lease was $400,000 (allegedly). Of this amount, $300,000 was covered by a nonrecourse "loan" secured by the mineral claim itself. Therefore, Meyers took an immediate $400,000 writeoff.

The tax deduction was based on IRC Section 616(a): *Development Expenditures*. This section reads in pertinent part—

> *There shall be allowed as a deduction . . . all expenditures paid or incurred during the taxable year for the development of a mine or other natural deposit . . . if paid or incurred **after the existence** of ores or minerals in **commercially marketable quantities** have been disclosed.* [Emphasis added.]

Thus, the basic reality issue was: Had the Meyers mine reached the development stage where commercially marketable quantities were known to exist?

In court, Meyers presented no factual evidence that any development work was ever performed on his mineral leased property. He offered two invoices, each for $200,000, stating: "Paid for development work." The invoices were not signed, nor did they describe the type or extent of development work. No reference was made whatsoever as to the existence of any amount of gold in his 250,000 cubic feet of gravel. The two paid invoices were forwarded to Meyers with a letter signed by M.M. Murphy, the principal agent for IME. The name M.M. Murphy was an alias for G.L. Rogers (real name) who used two other aliases: P.T. Smith and C.D. Blu. Testimony and documentation by the IRS showed that G.L. Rogers (the real person) was serving a 25-year prison sentence in Arizona for grand larceny.

When asked for backup documentation to support his $100,000 investment, Meyers offered only a photocopy of the front side of a check for $50,000. He did not produce the cancelled check to show that it actually had been negotiated.

Meyers alleged that $300,000 was a loan advanced to him by IME. The IRS submitted testimony and evidence that IME was a shell corporation. It had no assets; it had no monies to loan; it had no personnel; it had no workers or miners; it had no mining equipment; it had no license to operate in Panama; it had no mining leases of any kind; it had no survey maps of the area where the mining was to take place; it had no records of geological samples being taken to appraise the commercial viability of the operation.

What puzzled the court the most was why Meyers, who had a bachelor's degree in geology, never investigated the matter more intelligently. He never requested a professional assay of the auriferous gravel; he never requested a progress report on the development aspects; he never requested an accounting on his (alleged) $100,000 investment. He never inquired into the background and track record of the IME principals. He was totally blinded by the tax benefits, and he entered into the transaction solely for that reason.

Other Sham Cases

In *Meyers* above, it is — or should be — pretty obvious that the whole matter was a sham. Not only was no economic reality performed, there was no profit motive whatsoever. The only motivation was to get a tax writeoff . . . pure and simple.

The Meyers case is not unusual. Persons of means and intellect engage in various ventures which, on the surface at least, give the impression of being bona fide business activities. But when the underlying facts are investigated, the transactions are outright shams. To help you identify the kinds of activities involved, the following three cases are instructive. All are U.S. Appeals Court cases.

[1] *W.E. Gran*, U.S. Court of Appeals, 8th Circuit; 91-3150 EA, 5/21/92. Here, taxpayer Gran invested in a cattle breeding program of embryo transplants. He allegedly purchased 65 head of cattle, of which 25 were "superior" cows and 45 were regular cows. The superior cows were to be naturally impregnated by various species of superior bulls. After fertilization, the embryos were to be transplanted to the normal cows for bearing the newborn calves.

The purchase price of the 65 cows was $185,400 payable to Johnny Gardner Ranches in Missouri. Gran made a down payment of $18,500. Gardner was to be the manager of the program and was to solicit sales of the superior cows to other investors. The $166,900 balance of Gran's purchase price ($185,400 - $18,500) was to be paid out of sales of the superior cows and their transplanted calves.

What happened in reality?

Gardner never really sold any cows to Gran; Gardner retained his original ownership at all times. None of the cows were impregnated in any controlled manner. None of the "superior" cows were sold to new investors. There were no embryo transplants whatsoever. Gardner made no attempt to collect the $166,900 balance due on the alleged sale price. The court concluded that the purported sale to Gran was a sham, solely for the purpose of creating fictitious tax deductions.

[2] *J. Hildebrand, et al*, U.S. Court of Appeals, 9th Circuit, 91-70,030, 6/26/92. Here, taxpayer Hildebrand purchased a timeshare vacation home in Park City, Utah. The purchase price was $15,750. The contract called for a small down payment ($3,500) plus interest-only payments for 10 years. The balance of the principal and interest ($404,250) was due in a balloon payment at the end of 30 years. The contract was nonrecourse. This meant that Hildebrand could forfeit his timeshare units and avoid the final

payment. Meanwhile, for his downpayment year, Hildebrand took an accrued interest deduction of $25,290 on his tax return. This amount of deduction was more than seven times his down payment.

The court ruled that the nonrecourse debt was without economic substance. Although the condo unit was actually built, its fair market value (FMV) at time of purchase ($15,750) could not possibly have appreciated to the amount of the balloon payment ($404,250). Payments on principal yield no equity where the unpaid balance exceeds any current FMV. Consequently, the court concluded that the contract was a sham. No deductions of any kind were allowed.

[3] *J.F. Jackson*, U.S. Court of Appeals, 10th Circuit; 91-9017, 6/10/92. Here, taxpayer Jackson invested in a jewelry distribution franchise with exclusive, though unspecified, rights worldwide. The franchise was sold to Jackson by U.S. Distributors, Inc. whose subsidiary, American Gold & Diamond, was a manufacturer of gold jewelry and gems. After making a down payment of $15,000 on a $720,000 franchise, Jackson received an advisory statement that he could take a $60,000 deduction on his tax return (a 4-to-1 writeoff).

As it turned out, American Gold & Diamond had neither a ready supply of product, nor established goodwill. The company was founded and operated by the same persons responsible for U.S. Distributors. Thus, the court concluded that the worldwide exclusive rights had no economic substance and were in fact a sham.

Anatomy of a Sham

Sham cases are categorized as "generic (or abusive) tax shelters." They are classed this way because they all have certain characteristics in common.

The commonalty of character prevails whether there are art reproductions, jewelry franchises, or vacation timeshares involved. The taxpayer makes a down payment on a purchase price vastly in excess of the FMV of the property item offered. He invests his money without any foreknowledge of the activity, without expert advice, and without questioning the purchase price. The taxpayer's inquiries address the type and amount of tax benefits derived The courts have consistently ruled that tax motivated transactions are shams.

After many such rulings, the common characteristics of a sham have emerged. As a group, shams are identified by the following characteristics, namely:

(1)   tax benefits are the focus of promotional materials and sales pitches;
(2)   investors accept the terms of purchase without price negotiation;
(3)   the assets purchased are packages of purported rights, difficult to value in the abstract and substantially overvalued in relation to any tangible property included as part of the package;
(4)   tangible assets purchased, if any, are acquired or created at a relatively small cost shortly before being purchased by the investors; **and**
(5)   the bulk of the purchase price consideration is deferred by promissory notes, nonrecourse in form or in substance.

Because of the importance of the above characteristics, we are summarizing them in Figure 3.3. We want you to memorize Figure 3.3 and promise yourself that you will avoid such transactions

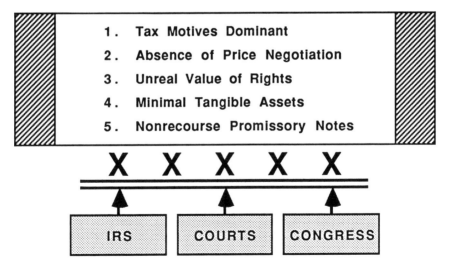

1.   Tax Motives Dominant

2.   Absence of Price Negotiation

3.   Unreal Value of Rights

4.   Minimal Tangible Assets

5.   Nonrecourse Promissory Notes

X   X   X   X   X

IRS   COURTS   CONGRESS

Fig. 3.3 - Characteristics of a Sham Transaction to Avoid

altogether. We also want you to know that there **is** a place for **bona fide** hobby business ventures, without any of the baggage of sham characterizations. You'll see this more in later chapters.

Quotable Judgments

As a hobby business venturer, it is important that you have a good grasp of the judicial sense that comes from case rulings. As you prepare to undertake your endeavors, the more you know about judicial wording and wisdom, the better you can stand up to the IRS when it — quite arbitrarily, in many cases — disallows your legitimate deductions. The bureaucratic mindset of the IRS marches to a different drummer. It is always under pressure to maximize revenue. It has very little calling to maximize justice.

For your preparatory guidance, we have culled through a number of recent court rulings on Section 183 to select a few which carry on objective message in succinct form. We present them below. We want you to read "between the lines." Upon doing so, you may acquire by osmosis the positive mode where you can prevail, should judicial scrutiny ever be turned on to you.

☐ A taxpayer's mere statement of intent is given less weight than objective facts.
— *Hines v. U.S.*, 912 F.2d 736-739 (4th Cir. 1990).

☐ When expert testimony does not withstand careful analysis, the Tax Court is not bound by such testimony, and may make a determination of . . . value based on its own evaluation of the evidence.
— *Lukens v. IRS*, 945 F.2d 96-99.

☐ In the face of a transaction which . . . was designated to produce tax benefits out of proportion with total investment, [such] facts do not establish the exercise of due care.
— *Sammons v. IRS*, 838 F.2d 330-337 (9th Cir.1991).

☐ Within the framework of a sham transaction, a taxpayer may incur bona fide obligations [where clearly separable] which should be recognized for tax purposes.
— *James v. IRS*, 899 F.2d 905-910 (10th Cir. 1990).

☐ The presence or absence of economic substance is determined by viewing the objective realities of the transaction, namely, whether what was actually done is what the parties to the transaction purported to do. — *Killingsworth v. IRS*, 864 F.2d 1214-1216 (5th Cir. 1989).

☐ Only a transaction that has economic substance which is compelled or encouraged by business or regulatory realities, and is imbued with tax-independent considerations, . . . will be recognized for tax purposes. — *Frank Lyon Co. v. U.S.*, 435 U.S. 561-584.

To capsulize the above, we list the following qualifications for threading your way through the always-lurking disallowance possibility:

- Due diligence,
- Separation of bona fides,
- Objective reality, and
- Tax-independent decisions.

Of these features, if we had to select only one for allowability-of-deduction success, it would be: making *tax-independent* decisions that further your enterprise.

Specialized Activities Best

We think that the best direction for Section 183 engagement is to focus on those activities which require highly specialized attention and follow-through. These are those activities where creativity, expertise, and perseverance are required. Applying specialized skills in a tax-independent manner automatically ascribes economic substance to the venture. If you do what you say you are going to do, and expend arm's-length money in the process, economic reality becomes self-evident.

By a "specialized activity," we mean the kind of venture that few other taxpayers do. It is the trial-and-error of starting and developing something new. You may do it on your own, in partnership with others, or as an independent investor in a small business corporation. The idea is that the undertaking is unusual; it has all the risks of success unknown. This very risk-taking feature — if you apply yourself diligently — is what makes your undertaking bona fide and genuine.

A good specialized case on point is that of *B.G. Persson*, TC Memo 1989-567. Taxpayer Persson bought a part-interest in a pedigreed, prize-winning Holstein bull. He and his co-owners sold the bull's semen to other registered Holstein cattle owners. In fact, they generated some $400,000 in semen sales over a period of several years. The expenses therewith, however, were greater than this amount. There were expenses of maintaining the bull (feeding, grooming, vetting), collecting and testing the semen, refrigerating it, transporting it, and impregnating it into fertile-tested and registered cows. Because there were substantial net losses, the IRS disallowed all expenses in excess of income [IRC Sec. 183(b)(2)].

Persson pursued the matter into Tax Court. The court overruled the IRS by concluding that Persson's undivided interest in the bull—

constituted an activity engaged in with an actual and honest profit objective.

Holding in Persson's favor, the court considered the following factors in reaching its decision:

(1)   the Holstein industry was riding the crest of record high prices for top pedigreed animals in the year the bull was purchased;
(2)   the individual was intimately acquainted with the registered Holstein cattle industry and had previously owned and operated a reputable dairy farm;
(3)   he had consulted an independent expert;
(4)   he was knowledgeable in the management and in the qualities necessary to develop a prize-winning dairy animal; and
(5)   the bull's semen generated over $400,000 in sales . . . which was not an insubstantial amount.

The key point in the *Persson* case is: The making of a net profit over several or many years is not, in and of itself, a prerequisite for establishing a profit motive. Many other factors must be taken into account.

4

PROFIT MOTIVE CRITERIA

The Courts And The IRS Have Devised 9 Objective Tests For Ascertaining If A Section 183 Activity Is Engaged In For Profit. The Most Prominent Tests Are The Amount Of TIME, EFFORT, And EXPERTISE Devoted To Your Venture. Also Important Is The Relative Absence Of Personal Pleasure And Recreation Therewith. Other INDICIA Of Profit Intentions Are Found In Regulations 1.183-2(a) [Activity Defined] And 1.183-2(b): [Relevant Factors]. Greater Weight Is Given To OBJECTIVE FACTS Than To Your Own Statement Of Intent.

In Chapter 2, we pointed out that Section 183 is "sandwiched" between Sections 162 and 212 of the IR Code. Section 162 (active trade or business) and Section 212 (property held for income) have been long recognized as profit-seeking endeavors. All related expenditures therewith are allowed, regardless of whether a net profit or net loss accrues for each taxable year. All other business-type activities are automatically swept into Section 183 as being not for profit.

In Chapter 3, we culled through many court cases weighing-in on Section 183. Those cases which received favorable judicial rulings were characterized by profit motive (Test A) and economic substance (Test B). Cases which failed both Test A and Test B were cited as shams. Though we did not always tell you so, each sham case provoked the court into imposing various penalties.

In the latter part of Chapter 3, we indicated that certain activities, because of their specialized nature and arm's-length financings, tend to automatically pass Test B (economic substance). These are those activities where specialized knowledge, expertise, and perseverance are required. These also are those activities where hands-on attention is required, and where financial and management decisions are made independently of any tax consequences. We see no point in your seeking the tax benefits of Section 183 if your basic transactions are not real, genuine, and straightforward. In other words, you direct your efforts at that type of activity where Test B (economic substance) is self-fulfilling.

This leaves the focus of this chapter on Test A: profit motive. What is this, and how is it objectively determined? Profit motive is *not* what you *say* it is. It is what your actions, behavior, and diligence towards your hobby business affairs reveal about your inner intentions. We want to lay these out for you in substantial detail.

Regulation 1.183-2(a)

Most sections of the Internal Revenue Code are backed up with regulatory clarifications. Purportedly, a regulation is to explain and clarify the meaning and intent of the key phrases in a tax law. This clarification does not always occur, but it is the purpose of a regulation nevertheless.

On this note we want to start with IRS Regulation 1.183-2(a). It is titled: **Activity not engaged in for profit defined;** *In General.* It is quite lengthy — about 300 words. We'll present it in two parts, separately, and add our interpretation of where the IRS is coming from.

The first part of Regulation 1.183-2(a) reads—

*For purposes of Section 183 . . ., the term "activity not engaged in for profit" means **any activity other than** one with respect to which deductions are allowable for the taxable year under section 162 or . . . section 212. Deductions are allowable under section 162 for expenses of **carrying on** activities which constitute a trade or business of the taxpayer and under section 212 for expenses **in connection with** activities engaged in for the production or collection of income or for the management, conservation, or maintenance of property held for the production of income. . . . Deductions are not allowable under section 162 or 212 for activities which are carried on primarily as a sport, hobby, or recreation. [Emphasis added.]*

This is an expansion of Section 183(c) which tells you that, if you are not in the livelihood endeavor of Sections 162 and 212, by definition you are in a not-for-profit endeavor. This does not mean that you have no profit motive. It simply means that you come under the provisions of Section 183 if you do not otherwise qualify under Sections 162 or 212. Particularly note that this part of the regulation expressly excludes sports, hobbies, or recreational-type activities.

The second part of Regulation 1.183-2(a) reads—

The determination on whether an activity is engaged in for profit is to be made by reference to objective standards, taking into account all of the facts and circumstances of each case. Although a reasonable expectation of profit is not required, the facts and circumstances must indicate that the taxpayer entered into the activity, or continued the activity, with the objective of making a profit. In determining whether such an objective exists, it may be sufficient that there is a small chance of making a large profit. . . . Greater weight is given to objective facts than to the taxpayer's mere statement of his intent. [Emphasis added.]

This portion of the regulation is trying to tell you that even if your activity is, by definition, Section 183 (not-for-profit), you may still get your losses deducted if your *objective* is to make a profit. Determining said objective is not based on your own statements of intent. It is based on all of the facts and circumstances of your entering into and continuing your activity.

"Relevant Factors" Listed

The objective criteria for determining your profit motive are listed in Regulation 1.183-2(b): *Relevant factors.* These are determinative factors which the various courts — over a period of many years — have agreed are indicative of your underlying motives. If you meet all of the qualifying tests, the presumption — for the year (or years) in question only — is that your activity is engaged in for profit. Whether you actually make a profit each year is another matter.

Like most regulations that the IRS promulgates, there is "weasel wording" in Reg. 1.183-2(b) that allows the IRS to disregard its own regulations when it wants to. The preamble to listing its relevant factor is a marvelous example of how the IRS weasel words a regulation.

There are **nine** relevant factors cited in Reg. 1.183-2(b). The preamble to this listing reads as follows:

> *In determining whether an activity is engaged in for profit, all facts and circumstances with respect to the activity are to be taken into account. No one factor is determinative in making this determination. In addition, it is not intended that only the factors described in this paragraph are to be taken into account . . ., or that a determination is to be made on the basis that the number of factors (whether or not listed in this paragraph) indicating a lack of profit objective exceeds the number of factors indicating a profit objective, or vice versa. Among the factors which should normally be taken into account are—*

What does this regulatory preamble say? It says that if five or more of the nine relevant factors are in your favor, your activity may still be judged as not-for-profit. The "vice versa" says that if you fail five or more of the nine factors, you could be judged for profit. This is the legalese way of saying that, although your profit motive is determined by nine objective factors, the determiner — the IRS or Tax Court (or other court) — can apply subjective analysis (personal judgment) when arriving at its conclusion. In other words, the nine factors are not tallied in scoreboard fashion, for determining your profit objectives.

What are the nine objective factors? In abbreviated fashion, they are listed in Figure 4.1 sequentially as they appear in Regulation 1.183-2(b)(1)-(9). We will address each factor separately.

Your Manner & Expertise

The first two factors in Figure 4.1 are captioned in Regulation 1.183-2(b) as follows:

(1)   Manner in which the taxpayer carries on the activity.

(2)   The expertise of the taxpayer or his advisors.

These two factors alone expose your inner genuineness before you yourself know it is being exposed.

More specifically, Regulation 1.183-2(b)(1): *Manner*, says—

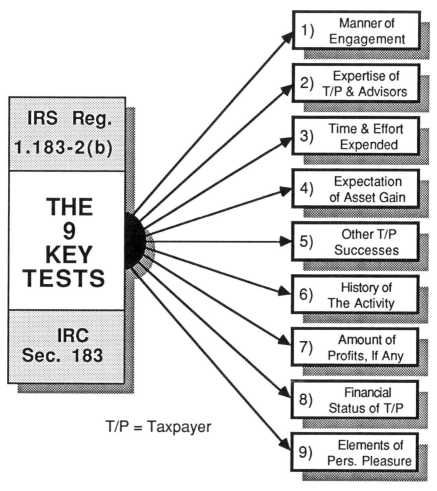

Fig. 4.1 - The "Relevant Factors" for Establishing Profit Motive

*The fact that the taxpayer carries on the activity in a businesslike manner and **maintains complete and accurate books** may indicate that the activity is engaged in for profit. Similarly, where an activity is carried on in a manner **substantially similar to other activities** of the same nature **which are profitable**, a profit motive may be indicated. A change of operating methods, adoption of new techniques or abandonment of unprofitable methods in a manner consistent with an intent to* *improve profitability may also indicate a profit motive.* [Emphasis added.]

All of which means that you have to carry on your hobby business activity as though you expected it to be profitable . . . someday. That is, you must conduct yourself in a businesslike manner, even though your activity is a spin-off from some sport, hobby, recreational, or side venture of your recent past. If you follow the practices of other similar hobby businesses which have made a profit, you are on the right track.

Supplementing your manner of operation is the expertise factor. On this, Regulation 1.183-2(b)(2): *Expertise*, says—

*Preparation for the activity by extensive study of its accepted business, economic, and scientific practices, or consultation with those who are expert therein, may indicate that the taxpayer has a profit motive where the taxpayer carries on the activity in accordance with such practices. Where a taxpayer has such preparation or procures such expert advice, but does not carry on the activity in accordance with such practices, a lack of intent to derive profit may be indicated unless it appears that the taxpayer is attempting to develop **new or superior techniques** which may result in profits from the activity.* [Emphasis added.]

This subregulation is telling you to prepare for your activity diligently, and follow "established practices" where they fit your situation. If you branch off into new and superior techniques, that's O.K., providing you have sought some expert advice on their feasibility. The whole idea is to demonstrate that you have the necessary savvy to run your hobby business prudently.

Time and Effort Expended

Factor (3) is captioned in Regulation 1.183-2(b) as follows:

(3) The time and effort expended by the taxpayer in carrying on the activity.

This particular factor is designed to assess your "devotion to duty." Its objective is to determine whether you are an active participant or a happy-go-lucky passive owner.

As to this factor, Regulation 1.183-2(b)(3): *Time and effort*, specifically says—

> *The fact that the taxpayer devotes much of his personal time and effort to carrying on an activity, particularly if the activity **does not have substantial personal or recreational aspects**, may indicate an intention to derive a profit. A taxpayer's withdrawal from another occupation to devote most of his energies to the activity may also be evidence that the activity is engaged in for profit. The fact that the taxpayer devotes a limited amount of time to an activity does not necessarily indicate a lack of profit motive where the taxpayer **employs competent and qualified persons** to carry on such activity.*
> [Emphasis added.]

The key concern of Test 3 is the amount of time and effort that you devote to the serious side of business, in contrast to the amount of personal pleasure and recreational benefits that you derive from it. If you expend more of your attention and energy on having a good time, rather than "minding the store," there is no way you can make a profit . . . ever. This one negative factor alone could defeat all of your other favorable profit-like endeavors.

It is not that you are prohibited from deriving any enjoyment from your hobby business; it is the nature of this enjoyment that is so revealing. If you enjoy the venture because it is challenging and offers the potential — somewhere down the line — of monetary rewards, that's fine. But if your attention to the affairs of state are more characterized by frivolity, sports, parties, travel, entertainment, and slipshod business practices, you have dug yourself firmly into the not-for-profit mold.

If your hobby business supplements in some connected way your livelihood occupation during its off-season, this will stand you well. In almost every livelihood business or occupation, there are off seasons, weekends, and spare moments that you can devote to your hobby business. Most livelihood business takes about 200 hours (for work and commute) of an average 720-hour month. If you devote whatever off-duty time and effort you have available to your Section 183 activity, in a serious and deliberate manner, this one factor alone could signify your for-profit intentions. So important is this time and effort concept that we depict our version of it in Figure 4.2.

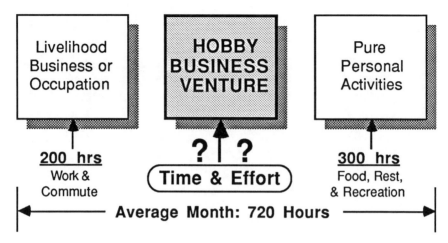

Fig. 4.2 - How Test 3 (Time & Effort) Is Evaluated

Expectation & Other Successes

Factors (4) and (5) are captioned in Regulation 1.183-2(b) as:

(4) Expectation that assets used in the activity may appreciate in value.

(5) The success of the taxpayer in carrying on other similar or dissimilar activities.

These two factors are designed to test your ordinary business acumen. With respect to profits made elsewhere, if any, did you make good business decisions? Or, are you cavalier about financial and tax matters?

As to factor (4) — Test 4 — Regulation 1.183-2(b)(4): *Expectation of appreciation*, reads as follows:

The term "profit" encompasses appreciation in the value of the assets, such as land, used in the activity. Thus, the taxpayer may intend to derive profit from the operation of the activity, and may also intend that, even if no profit from current operations is derived, an overall profit will result when appreciation in value of the land . . . is realized, since income from the activity, together with the appreciation of land will exceed expenses of operation.

This test assumes that, if you use ordinary business prudence, you'll acquire appreciation-type assets (land, buildings, franchises, goodwill, licenses, etc.) at competitive market values. If the assets do appreciate in value, and you sell, you are bound to make some profit, called "capital gain." Even the someday expectation of capital gain is indicative of your profit motivation. If your hobby business does not require the acquisition of appreciation-type assets, then, of course, Test 4 does not apply.

As to Test 5, Regulation 1.183-2(b)(5): *Other successes*, reads in full as—

The fact that the taxpayer has engaged in similar activities in the past and converted them from unprofitable to profitable enterprises may indicate that he is engaged in the present activity for profit, even though the activity is presently unprofitable.

This test says that if you have operated a similar — or even dissimilar — business in the past, and it was profitable at some point, you probably intend to turn a profit in your current activity. In other words, your sound business judgment in the past is considered transferable to your current and future businesses. If you have had no prior similar/dissimilar business experience, your current profit potential is indeterminable.

History of Income & Losses

If you have been engaged in your current (hobby business) activity for a number of years before being challenged by the IRS, factor (6) — Test 6 — is a comprehensive review of your efforts therewith. This test is captioned in Regulation 1.183-2(b) as follows—

(6) The taxpayer's history of income or losses with respect to the activity.

The phrase "with respect to **the** activity" means the current activity only. It does not include any prior activities considered in Test 5.

Subregulation 1.183-2(b)(6): *History of income*, reads:

*A series of losses during the initial or start-up stage of an activity may not necessarily be an indication that the activity is not engaged in for profit. However, where losses continue to be sustained **beyond the period which customarily is necessary** to bring the operation to profitable status such continued losses, if not explainable, as due to customary business risks or reverses, may be indicative that the activity is not being engaged in for profit. If losses are sustained because of **unforeseen or fortuitous circumstances** which are beyond the control of the taxpayer, such as drought, disease, fire, theft, weather damages, other involuntary conversions, or depressed market conditions, such losses would not be an indication that the activity is not engaged in for profit. A series of years in which net income was realized would of course be strong evidence that the activity is engaged in for profit.* [Emphasis added.]

Test 6 is your best opportunity to explain your trials and tribulations of a long series of loss years. Do you recall that Section 183(d) [Chapter 2] — the presumption rule — accepts only two loss years in a consecutive period of five years? If for some reason other than not-for-profit, you have suffered five consecutive loss years, you have some convincing explaining to do.

Explaining a long series of losses is best achieved by characterizing them as three separate types or classes (as depicted in Figure 4.3). Type I losses are those occurring during your initial startup years. Type II losses are those due to unforeseen and uncontrolled events. Type III losses are those which occur after one or more consecutive profit years. If you experience Types I, II, and III losses consecutively, you'll have real difficulty explaining them!

In most new business startups, it takes about three years to get into the profit-making mode. Section 183(d) allows only two years. Two years is a little unrealistic. Therefore, we interpret these two years as two *full* 12-month years after a part-year which is your startup year. A "part-year" is less than 12 months (obviously). It is "customary" to lose money in the first couple of years of any new business, be it hobby or for livelihood.

If **other than** during the startup years — such as Types II or III in Figure 4.3 — you have three loss years in a row, you had better have good explanations. There may have been a major fire, earthquake or flood where your business premises are located. There may have been an airport or highway expansion project which

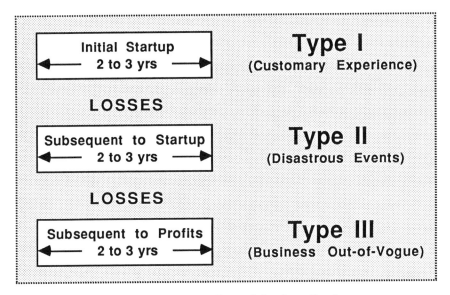

Initial Startup
◄——— 2 to 3 yrs ———►

Type I
(Customary Experience)

LOSSES

Subsequent to Startup
◄——— 2 to 3 yrs ———►

Type II
(Disastrous Events)

LOSSES

Subsequent to Profits
◄——— 2 to 3 yrs ———►

Type III
(Business Out-of-Vogue)

Fig. 4.3 - The "Loss Types" In Any Business

cut off ready access to your business premises. Your product or service suddenly went out of vogue For example, you may have been selling sports paraphernalia endorsing your home team, and the home team moves to a distant geographic area.

Whatever really took place in the Phase II and Phase III loss years, you had better have good documentation. For this purposes, appropriate photographs, newspaper articles, legal filings, insurance claims, police records, health and safety inspections, etc. will be most helpful. Otherwise, any "sad story" you tell will be disbelieved. All Section 183 losses are basically a No-No, except in the first few startup years.

Occasional Profits & Status

There is one basic idea behind allowing any Section 183 losses, whether startup or otherwise. There has to be a vision, some hope, some evidence of making a profit, somewhere down the line. Towards this end, occasional profits and the financial status of the taxpayer are important test considerations. This is where factors (7) and (8) come into play. These two factors/tests are captioned in Regulation 1.183-2(b) as—

(7) The amount of occasional profits, if any, which are earned.

(8) The financial status of the taxpayer.

As to Test 7, Regulation 1.183-2(b)(7): *Occasional profits*, reads as—

*The amount of profits **in relation to the amount of losses incurred,** and **in relation to the amount of the taxpayer's investment** and the value of the assets used in the activity, may provide useful criteria in determining the taxpayer's intent. An occasional small profit from an activity generating large losses, or from an activity in which the taxpayer has made a large investment, would not generally be determinative that the activity is engaged in for profit. However, **substantial profit, though only occasional,** would generally be indicative that an activity is engaged in for profit, where the investment or losses are comparatively small. Moreover, an opportunity to earn a substantial ultimate profit in **a highly speculative venture** is ordinarily sufficient to indicate that the activity is engaged in for profit even though losses or only occasional small profits are actually generated.* [Emphasis added.]

There you have it! You have got to show some profit, or real profit potential, at some time in the whole course of your venture. Never ever having a profit just won't fly.

As to Test 8, Regulation 1.183-2(b)(8): *Financial status*, reads—

The fact that the taxpayer does not have substantial income or capital from sources other than the activity may indicate that an activity is engaged in for profit. Substantial income from sources other than the activity (particularly if the losses from the activity generate substantial tax benefits) may indicate that the activity is not engaged in for profit. . . .

Test 8 pretty well spotlights the nature of a hobby business venture. As we have stated earlier (probably several times), a hobby business is a side business. It is separate and apart from one's livelihood activity. Any substantial disparity between the two incomes may be indicative of not-for-profit motives.

What the IRS is really targeting in Test 8 are the relative tax benefits between your hobby business and livelihood activities. The central message is that if your hobby business benefits are too great, you are more motivated by tax reasons than by profit reasons. This is a precursor for citing your Section 183 activity as a sham.

Elements of Personal Pleasure

Actually, we omitted above the very last phrase in Test 8. That regulatory phrase is

. . . especially if there are personal or recreational elements involved.

This phrase is an overlap and tie-in with the last and final relevant factor, namely: Test 9. Test 9 is captioned in Regulation 1.183-2(b) as—

(9) Elements of personal pleasure or recreation.

This test is almost self-explanatory, but not fully so.

As to factor (9), Regulation 1.183-2(b)(9): *Elements of pleasure*, reads in essential part as—

*The presence of personal motives in carrying on of an activity may indicate that the activity is not engaged in for profit, especially where there are recreational or personal elements involved. On the other hand, a profit motivation may be indicated where an activity lacks any appeal other than profit. It is not, however, necessary that an activity be engaged in with the exclusive intention of deriving a profit or with the intention of maximizing profits. . . . **An activity will not be treated as not engaged in for profit merely because the taxpayer has purposes or motivations other than solely to make a profit.** Also, the fact that the taxpayer derives personal pleasure from engaging in the activity is not sufficient to cause the activity to be classed as not engaged in for profit if the activity is in fact engaged in for profit as evidenced by other factors . . . [listed above]. [Emphasis added.]*

Test 9 is really the "wrap-up" test of the evidence that comes forth from Tests 1 through 8. In other words, the IRS considers the extent and degree of personal pleasure in an activity as the strongest indicator of your true motivation therewith. It is not that all personal pleasure and recreational elements are prohibited. It is that such pleasure and recreation, if any, must be subordinated to the longer term objective of deriving a respectable profit somewhere in the course of time. The fact that you may not really enjoy your hobby business, but you participate in it nevertheless, is a good indication of motives other than pleasure and recreation.

No matter how many profit motive tests (criteria) you pass or fail, Test 9 is usually the clincher when your hobby business comes under scrutiny. This test silently permeates all others.

Example of No Pleasure

Typically, scrutiny of your Section 183 activity goes like this. After proper notice from the IRS, an examination of returns for three or more years takes place. During the examination, it is noted that your primary occupation or other livelihood endeavors generate substantial positive income. It is also noted that your hobby business venture generates negative income (net losses) for two or more years. To the IRS, this makes it obvious that you are using your Section 183 losses to offset your livelihood positive income for the corresponding years. We depict this "classical" arrangement in Figure 4.4. Because the federal tax you paid is lower than it would have been without the hobby business, IRS scrutiny follows to see if it can disallow your hobby losses altogether.

In a pertinent recent case (settled out of court), the taxpayer was a real estate agent: an unmarried woman whom we'll call "Mary." Mary happened to own 50 head of cattle which she grazed on rental pasture land. She had been doing this for four years (all at losses) when the IRS stepped in.

The IRS auditor asserted that none of Mary's cattle losses were allowable. He wrote to Mary saying—

"From the information you have provided, the only alternative for me to conclude is that your cattle raising venture is not engaged in for profit. Under IRS Code rules, a business must show a profit in 3 of 5 consecutive years. If you do show a profit in the coming years, you may be able to overcome the decision at this time.

/s/
IRS Auditor"

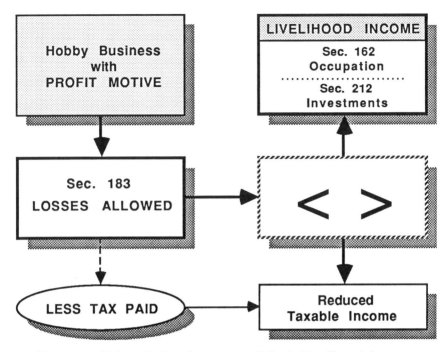

Fig. 4.4 - Using Hobby Losses to Offset Livelihood Income

Included with the above disallowance statement was a tax bill for $15,130 **Balance Due** . . . with penalties.

Mary prepared a 4-page typewritten protest and response. Her preamble/introductory paragraph read—

"You have erred in your interpretation and application of Code Sec.183. You have made a subjective inference rather than an objective analysis of all facts and circumstances surrounding the case. Sec. 183 applies to . . . *those activities which are carried on primarily as a sport, hobby, or for recreation.* [Reg. 1.183-2(a).]   There is no sport, hobby, or recreational aspect whatsoever to the branding, feeding, calving, vaccination, culling, carting dead carcasses, and shoveling manure for 50 head of commercial cattle and their calves. These are not house pets and they cannot be raced for sport or ridden for pleasure.

"Reg. 1.183-2(b) states quite specifically that . . . *No one factor is determinative . . . in determining whether an activity is engaged in for profit.* You have considered net operating losses only . . . and no other factors."

Mary then went on to cite all nine of the factors above, and filled in the pertinent facts and circumstances. In reality, Mary was born and reared on a farm. She married a cattle rancher and assisted him until she was divorced. She then assisted a 70-year-old cattle ranching friend, from whom she bought the 50 head of cattle for her own enterprise.

Some six months later, Mary received an official notification from her local IRS District Director. The letter said—

We are pleased to tell you that our examination of your tax returns for the above periods show **no change is necessary** *in your reported tax* [as originally filed]. [Emphasis added.]

Thus you see: If you pass the scrutiny tests of Reg. 1.183-2(b): *Profit Motive Criteria*, you **can** be allowed your Section 183 losses. In Mary's case, this was four loss years in a row.

5

TAX FORMS INVOLVED

Using The Appropriate Tax Forms And Schedules Can Materially Ease Your 1040 Return Through IRS's Intricate Computer Processing System. For Claiming Operating Expenses, Use Schedules C, E, F And Form 4835. For Claiming Depreciation, Use Form 4562. For Computing Gain Or Loss Upon Disposition Of Assets, Use Schedule D And Form 4797. For Computing The Limitations On The Losses You Can Claim, Use Forms 6198 (At Risk) And 8852 (Loss Carryovers). For Entering Your Prorata Share From Partnerships And S Corporations, Schedules K-1 Are Required. These K-1's "Dovetail" Into Schedule E (Part II) To Join Other Attachments To Your Form 1040.

One key to success in the allowability of your hobby business losses is the tax form, or forms, that you use. If you use the right forms, use them properly, and use them consistently, you have a much better chance of your Section 183 activity passing through the system unscrutinized.

As you may or may not know, human eyes at the IRS processing centers rarely look at and read tax returns. Everything today is done electronically — computer scanning, computer processing, computer matching, and computer selecting. The IRS's in-house computer programs are keyed directly to the tax forms (which the IRS designs) and to specific line numbers on each form. If you make the proper line entries and use the correct form (for your type of activity), the forms themselves become your general passport to acceptance.

This is not to say that using the proper tax forms correctly will always pass through the system unnoticed. The IRS is more computer sophisticated than this. But, you have a far better chance of avoiding scrutiny if you do your tax reportings correctly, whether they be losses or profits.

In this chapter, therefore, we want to describe very briefly the essential forms that you will need. Emphasis is on those forms and schedules which attach to your personal Form 1040: *U.S. Individual Income Tax Return.* Of course, not all of the forms we present will apply to your particular hobby business. But, if you change hobby businesses from time to time, or if you engage in multiple separate activities concurrently, sooner or later most of the forms we describe will require your attention.

Overview of 1040 Schedules

The lower half of page 1 of your Form 1040 lists 16 classes of income which you must report, as applicable. Each source-class of income is entered on a separate line of its own. If you have several incomes from the same source-class, you enter only the summary of that income.

The 16 separate summaries entered on page 1 address your livelihood income, investment income, business income, pension income, entitlement income, and any other income sources. There are no special entry lines for hobby business matters. Therefore, you have to adapt certain lines which are keyed to Section 162 businesses and Section 212 investments. There are five such lines as follows:

1. Business income or <loss>   [attach **Schedule C**]
2. Capital gain or <loss>   [attach **Schedule D**]
3. Other gains or <losses>   [attach **Form 4797**]
4. Rents, royalties, partnerships, etc. [attach **Schedule E**]
5. Farm income or <loss>   [attach **Schedule F**]

Caution: The actual line numbers on your Form 1040 differ from the above, but the sequence and wording is the same as we have listed. Their relative location on Form 1040 is as we depict in Figure 5.1. There are also other forms and schedules which supplement those highlighted in Figure 5.1.

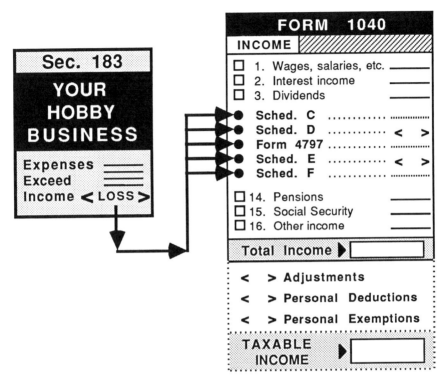

Fig. 5.1 - How Hobby Business Activities "Fit" On Form 1040

If you are inclined to complain about attaching supplemental forms and schedules to your 1040 and want to skip them, you can do so. In such case, you simply add up all income and proceeds reported to you on various "information returns" and on other payer statements. Then enter the grand total on the last income entry line on page 1 of your 1040 which reads—

*Other income (list type and amount)*_____

When you do this, you realize, of course, that you have no way of claiming your Section 183 expenses, deductions, credits, and other allowances. The net consequence is that you pay the maximum possible tax. Therefore, if you detest filling out supplemental tax forms, your only alternative is to pay maximum tax.

HOBBY BUSINESS VENTURES

Schedule C (Form 1040)

Schedule C (1040) is titled: ***Profit or Loss From Business*** (Sole Proprietorship). A headnote instruction says: *Attach to Form 1040; See Instructions.* The first paragraph of the instructions reads in part—

> *If you operated a business or practiced a profession as a sole proprietorship, complete Schedule C. If you had more than one business, or if you and your spouse had separate businesses, you must complete a Schedule C for each business. Do not report gambling winnings on Schedule C unless you are a professional gambler.*

Probably any hobby business venture is a form of gambling. Although Schedule C is not specifically intended for hobby businesses, it can be used for such, if your Section 183 activity fits into any one of the 185 business types for which Schedule C is designed. Schedule C is intended primarily for Section 162-type business where products or services are sold, including research, mining, publishing, lodging, recreation, travel, transportation, apparel, games, etc. It cannot be used for animal breeding, farming, property rentals, partnership ventures, or the sale of capital assets.

On the reverse side of Schedule C, there is a listing of the 185 different types of businesses that can be accommodated on the front Each of these 185 activities is assigned a 4-digit code. The instructions tell you to—

> *Locate the major category that best describes your activity. Within the major category, select the activity code that most closely identifies the business or profession that is the principal source of your sales or receipts. Enter this 4-digit code in box B on page 1* [of Schedule C].

Care in selecting the proper 4-digit code which "most closely identifies" your hobby business will materially aid in the IRS's computer acceptance of your Schedule C as filed.

For example, suppose you are a golf enthusiast who has developed a special club for getting out of sand traps, water ponds, and thick underbrush. You manufacture and sell these under your own brand name: "Sand Traps No More." Among the 185 codified businesses on the reverse side of Schedule C, you would find under

Miscellaneous Retail activities: *Sporting goods & bicycle shops.*
For this, the assigned 4-digit code is "4679." You would enter this
number as well as your business name in the upper portion of
Schedule C. You would enter—

Mfg. & Sales: specialty golf clubs: 4679
dba: Sand Traps No More [the "dba" is: doing business as]

For introductory and overview purposes only, we present in
Figure 5.2 the general format and contents of Schedule C. It
consists of nearly 50 separate entry lines plus three supplemental
forms. A quick glance at this figure is all you need at this time. As
we get into specific hobby business examples in later chapters, we'll
expand on the portions of Schedule C that are pertinent at that time.

Schedule D (Form 1040)

Schedule D (1040) is titled: ***Capital Gains and Losses.*** A
small headnote says: *Attach to Form 1040; See Instructions.*
The leadoff instructions say in pertinent part—

Use Schedule D to:

• *Report the sale or exchange of a capital asset* [such as]
  (a) *proceeds from transactions involving stocks, bonds,
    and other securities, and*
  (b) *gross proceeds from real estate transactions not
    reported on another form or schedule.*
• *Report gains from involuntary conversions of capital assets
  not held for business or profit.*
• *Reconcile Forms 1099-B you got for bartering transactions.*

The whole idea of Schedule D is to report every transaction you
make involving a capital asset, whether used in business or not.
The term "capital asset" means virtually any item of property that
you own and use for personal purposes, pleasure, business, or
investment. If you sell an asset that has been used in your hobby
business (such as vehicles, equipment, machinery, or structures), it
is reported on Form 4797 (Sales of Business Property) before being
reported on Schedule D.
   If you make, say, 35 sales, exchanges, or other transactions
involving capital assets during the year, you must report **each one**

Sch.C (1040)	PROFIT OR LOSS FROM BUSINESS	Year

BUSINESS NAME, PRODUCT, SERVICE	B	Principle Activity Code (4-digits)

☐ **Material participation?** Accounting method ☐ ☐ ☐
Inventory method ☐ ☐ ☐

Part I	INCOME	About 6 entry lines
Part II	EXPENSES	About 20 entry lines

● Other expenses (list type and amount)

Part III	COST OF GOODS	About 6 entry lines

● Other costs (list type and amount)

Net Profit or Loss ▶   4 computational lines PLUS foot note instructions ☐ ☐

Supplemental Forms (As Applicable)

☐ **4562** - Depreciation & Amortization

☐ **6198** - At-Risk Limitations

☐ **8829** - Expenses for Business Use of Home

☐ **Sch. SE** - Self-Employment Tax (Soc. Sec.)

Fig. 5.2 - Abbreviated Contents of Schedule C   (1040)

separately. For this purpose, there is a separate entry line for each transaction. If there are not enough entry lines on the face of Schedule D, there is a Continuation Sheet: Schedule D-1. Schedules D and D-1 can accommodate up to 50 short-term transactions and up to 50 long-term transactions. The distinction between "short term" and "long term" has to do with holding period: one year or less, or more than one year.

Most hobby business venturers overlook the importance of Schedule D when they have capital losses. If the losses can be characterized as being derived from bona fide investment-type assets, in contrast to personal or recreational assets, they can "fit onto" Schedule D as: *Other Transactions*. On both the short-term and long-term subschedules, there are three entry lines for those transactions which are not generally reported to the IRS. These nondescript entry lines could be used more often by hobby venturers than is presently the case.

Form 4797: Highly Versatile

A special capital gain/ordinary loss tax form that applies only to businesses — including hobby businesses — is **Form 4797**. It is titled: *Sales of Business Property (Also Involuntary Conversions and Recapture Amounts)*. "Involuntary conversions" are those induced by eminent domain or by the threat thereof. "Recapture amounts" are the recovery of depreciation allowances, expense elections, and tax benefits previously allowed on certain property items (computers, cellular phones, autos, entertainment facilities) when their business use drops to 50% or less.

Form 4797 is the most versatile tax form that we know of. For business owners and investors, it is designed to accommodate those transactions (sales, exchanges, abandonment, etc.) involving—

1. Depreciable tangible property (machinery, equipment)
2. Amortizable intangible items (startup costs, customer lists)
3. Depreciable realty structures
4. Depreciable residential rentals
5. Oil, gas, geothermal, & mineral rights
6. Farmland held less than 10 years
7. Preproductive vineyards and orchards
8. Agricultural cost-sharing property
9. Cattle & horses: draft, breeding, dairy, or sporting
10. Livestock other than cattle & horses
11. Casualties, disasters, & thefts
12. Section 1231 property items

The greatest value of Form 4797 to hobby business venturers is its special rule for Section 1231 property. This IR Code section is titled: **Property Used in the Trade or Business and Involuntary Conversions.** The essence of this rule is that upon the disposition of used business assets—

☐ If gains exceed the losses, the net gain shall be treated as long-term capital gain (reportable on Schedule D).

☐ If losses exceed the gains, the net loss shall be treated as an ordinary/noncapital loss (deductible against other positive income on page 1 of Form 1040).

In effect, Section 1231 is: Heads you win; tails you also win. It gives you the best of both tax worlds: the gains world and the loss world. Capital gains are taxed more favorably than ordinary gains. Ordinary losses are more tax beneficial than capital losses. If you will remember this one win-win feature alone (of Section 1231 via Form 4797), you will enjoy special tax benefits rarely known to other Section 183 venturers.

The versatility of Form 4797 as it relates to Schedule D and Form 1040 is presented in Figure 5.3. As you will note, Part III of Form 4797 addresses certain "recapture property" which is best described in the official instructions. The form, on separate lines in Parts I and II, also accepts like-kind exchanges, installment sales, casualties and thefts, listed property (mixed use: business-personal), and various "other transactions" (by partnerships and S corporations). The rule of thumb is that *when in doubt* concerning disposition of Section 183 assets, **use Form 4797.** Many tax accounting matters can fit on this form, when they cannot fit on other forms and schedules.

Schedule E (Form 1040)

Schedule E (1040) is titled: *Supplemental Income and Loss (From Rental Real Estate, Royalties, Partnerships, Estates, Trusts, Etc.).* This schedule is partitioned into three distinctive parts, namely:

Part I   Income or Loss from Rental Real Estate and Royalties (from oil, gas, or mineral properties; copyrights, and patents). [Instructions caution against using this part to report income and expenses from the rental of vehicles, machinery, equipment, and farmland.]

Part II   Income or Loss from Partnerships and S Corporations.

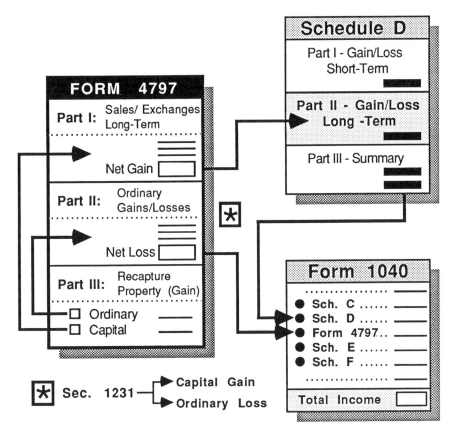

Fig. 5.3 - Use of Form 4797 When Disposing of Business Assets

Part III Income or Loss from Estates and Trusts. [There is not much likelihood that an estate or trust would intentionally engage in Section 183-type activities.]

Part I of Schedule E, rents and royalties, accommodates up to three property rentals including vacation and recreational residential facilities. If more than three properties are involved, add additional schedules and mark them sequentially as E-1, E-2, E-3, etc. The same applies to royalty properties, where payments are made based on the productivity of the lessee (tenant).

Part I of Schedule E takes up the entire front (page 1). The general format is in three sections, namely: Income, Expenses, and

Loss Limitations. There are just two income entry lines: one for rents received (including security deposits, laundry machine receipts, etc.) and one for royalties received. Income from rental and royalty property derives primarily from the large capital investment in the property, as distinguished from personal service income entered on Schedule C.

The expense section of Part I consists of some 15 preprinted entry lines. The preprinted expense categories span the gamut of advertising, auto & travel, depreciation, repairs, utilities, etc. These are the customary types of expenditures that every property owner incurs when renting or leasing his property to others.

If you own multiple rental/royalty properties such as A, B, C, etc., you cannot aggregate the income and expenses for entry on Schedule E. For each expense category, you must allocate separately the income and expenses for property A, for property B, for property C, and so on. The reason for this is that each property (which is separately titled and recorded) is capable of being sold or exchanged on its own. When this happens, the history of income, expenses, and loss carryovers, if any, needs to be separately traceable to each property.

The loss limitations section of Part I calls for the preparation (as applicable) of Form 6198 (At-Risk Limitations) and Form 8582 (Passive Activity Loss Limitations). All rental real estate, limited partnerships, and S corporations are classed as "passive activities." Passive activities require the preparation of loss limitations Forms 6198 and 8582, whereas nonpassive activities do not.

Part II of Schedule E, partnerships and S corporations, requires information from another schedule — called: Schedule K-1 — before any entries can be made. The information from the K-1 allocates your prorata share of the income or loss between passive and nonpassive activities. Nonpassive partnerships and S corporations are those in which you participate actively (over 100 hours) or materially (over 500 hours) each year.

Schedules K-1 (Forms 1065/1120S)

Schedule K-1 (1065) is titled: *Partner's Share of Income, Credits, Deductions, Etc.* This is a spin-off from Form 1065 which is titled: U.S. Partnership Share of Income. The K-1 is prepared by the "Tax Matters Partner" and is sent separately to each member of the partnership There are approximately 200 different types of partnership businesses recognized for tax purposes.

Schedule K-1 (Form 1120S) is titled: ***Shareholder's Share of Income, Credits, Deductions, Etc.*** This is a spin-off from Form 1120S which is titled: U.S. Income Tax Return for an S Corporation. This K-1 is prepared by a "Tax Matters Person" and also is sent separately to each shareholder in the S corporation. There also are about 200 different types of S corporation businesses recognized for tax purposes.

At the headpart of the partnership K-1, there are 10 questions and check-boxes citing pass-through information on each partner. For example, one question/statement says—

Enter partner's percentage of:
Profit sharing _____%
Loss sharing _____%
Ownership of capital _____%
Share of liabilities _____%

In contrast, the S corporation K-1 merely cites—

Shareholder's percentage of stock ownership _____%

Otherwise, page 1 of the partnership K-1 and that of the S corporation are virtually identical. Each consists of approximately 30 entry lines, arranged in three columns. Column (a) identifies the source of income, loss, deduction, credits, interest expense, etc. Column (b) lists the dollar amount applicable. Column (c) directs the distributee as to what form and what schedule he/she is to enter and attach to his/her own Form 1040 return. Instructions caution each recipient NOT to attach the K-1 to his return, as the IRS already has the K-1 information.

Page 2 of the partnership K-1 and that of the S corporation also is essentially identical. It consists of about 15 preprinted entries (adjustments, foreign taxes, recapture items) plus about a half-page of blank space for supplemental information. Instructions caution each participant to keep track of his/her own tax basis accounting. That is, each member has to keep track of his own contributory share to the entity, and his increases or decreases at the end of each K-1 year. Each member is also required to do his own accounting when his interest in the entity is terminated.

Partnerships and S corporations are advantageous for hobby businesses where the resources needed (money, talent, and equipment) exceed the capabilities of an individual entrepreneur and his closest associates. Activities involving research, experimentation, exploration, drilling, and mining are among the best candidates for entity ventures.

Schedule F (Form 1040)

Schedule F (1040) is titled: *Profit or Loss From Farming*. It is intended for those who "materially participate" in farming and agricultural activities. An instructional caution on the form says to use Schedule C if—

- *Your principal source of income is from providing agricultural services such as soil preparation, veterinary, farm labor, horticultural, or management for a fee or on a contract basis, or*
- *You are engaged in the business of breeding, raising, and caring for dogs, cats, or other pet animals.*

Otherwise, Schedule F is intended for those activities involving field crops, fruit and nuts, hogs and sheep, beef cattle, dairy products, poultry and eggs, specialty animals (horses, bees, snakes, fur-bearing, etc.), forest products, and general livestock. Altogether, there are 15 such tax recognized agricultural activities. Each is identified by a 3-digit code (listed on the reverse side of Schedule F) which is a required entry on page 1, just above the 10-line entry for farm income.

There are about 25 entry lines on Schedule F with preprinted expense categories. Because farming involves a lot of personal living off of the land, the Schedule F instructions state quite emphatically—

Do not deduct:
- *Personal or living expenses (such as taxes, insurance, or repairs on your home) that do not produce farm income.*
- *Expenses of raising anything you or your family used.*
- *The value of animals you raised that died.*
- *Loss of inventory and personal losses.*
- *Depreciation on your home, furniture, or car.*

As a hobby business farmer, you have to be particularly careful to avoid the impression that you are enjoying personal benefit from your agricultural activities. There is no point in your risking disallowance of the many tax benefits that Schedule F provides.

Form 4835: Farm Rental

A tax form closely similar to that of Schedule F is Form 4835. It is titled: *Farm Rental Income and Expenses.* It carries the subtitle: *Crop and Livestock Shares (Not Cash) Received by Landowner (or Sub-Lessor).* The key difference between Form 4835 and Schedule F is that any net income from farm rentals is NOT subject to the self-employment tax. This feature alone makes Form 4835 more attractive to hobby farmers than Schedule F.

The idea behind Form 4835 is sharecrop farming. That is, you own a certain number of acres of farmland. You rent or lease your land, buildings, and equipment, if any, to real down-to-earth farmers. Instead of collecting fixed monthly rent in the form of money, you collect a share (typically 35%) of the crop, livestock, fruit & nuts, etc. that the tenant farmer produces. For tax and legal reasons, a Sharecropping Agreement (in the form of a lease) is signed by you as the landlord and by the tenant farmer. In some rural areas, it is customary for the landowner to provide a place of residence for the tenant and his family.

The tipoff that there is a Section 183 distinction between Form 4835 and Schedule F lies in comparing one particular headnote question on each of the forms. On Form 4835, you are asked:

Did you "actively participate" in the operation of this farm?

On Schedule F, you are asked:

Did you "materially participate" in the operation of this business?

Active participation means only that you manage and oversee the farm property that you own. Material participation is more of a hands-on, day-to-day engagement in farming as a livelihood. Farming as a livelihood has no attraction for hobby venturers. In contrast, farm rentals via sharecropping are highly attractive.

The instructions to Form 4835 define "active participation" as—

You are considered to actively participate if you participated in making management decisions or arranging for others to provide services (such as repairs) in a significant and bona fide sense.

Management decisions that are relevant in this context include approving new tenants, deciding on rental terms, approving capital or repair expenditures, and other similar decisions. You do not, however, actively participate if at any time during the year your interest (including your spouse's interest in the activity) was less than 10% (by value) of all interests in the activity.

Thus, for hobby business purposes, it is more practical and realistic to be a Form 4835-type farmer than a Schedule F type. Insofar as income and expenses are concerned, Form 4835 and Schedule F are nearly identical. For a functional understanding of the difference between Form 4835 and Schedule F, we present Figure 5.4.

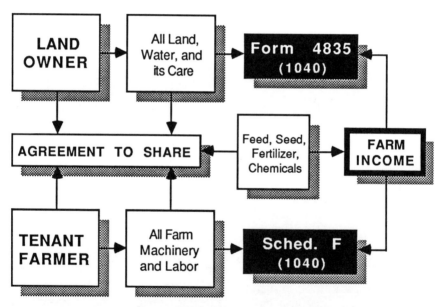

Fig. 5.4 - Tax Form Differences When Renting Farmland

Form 4562: Depreciation

Of the forms introduced above, Schedules C, E, F, and Form 4835 all permit the claiming of a depreciation allowance on those capital assets used in the business. For computing the correct amount of depreciation allowable, Form 4562 is required. This form is titled: *Depreciation and Amortization (Including Information on Listed Property)*. The term "listed property" refers to mixed-use assets such as automobiles, computers, recreational items, etc.

Form 4562 is a very comprehensive 2-page form with approximately 60 entry lines. It is designed primarily to spotlight those assets placed in service during the current year. Those assets placed in service in prior years are "kept track of" on a *Depreciation Worksheet* which supplements Form 4562. Over 8,000 words of official instructions (6 pages, 3 columns wide) accompany the form.

Form 4562 is arranged in six parts as follows:

Part I   — Election to Expense Section 179 Property
Part II   — MACRS Depreciation: Current Year
Part III   — Other Depreciation: Prior Years
Part IV   — Summary (of Parts I, II, III, and V)
Part V   — Listed Property & Vehicle Information
Part VI   — Amortization (of Certain Intangible Assets)

A quick review of each part, except the summary, is in order.

Part I allows you to take advantage of the $10,000 "expense election" of Section 179 (Certain Depreciable Business Assets) of the tax code. This election applies only to those vehicles, machinery, tools, and equipment *acquired by purchase* for use in your business activities. As per subsection 179(b)(3)(A), the amount of the $10,000 deduction that you can take—

> *... shall not exceed the aggregate amount of the taxable income of the taxpayer for such taxable year which is derived from the **active conduct** of the taxpayer **of any trade or business** during such taxable year.* [Emphasis added.]

In other words, even though your hobby business may show a loss, if you are actively employed or self-employed in a livelihood business, you can use your livelihood business income to qualify you for the Section 179 election.

Part II, MACRS depreciation, lists six tangible property classes and two real property classes for claiming the first-year's depreciation on your newly acquired assets. Incidentally, the letters MACRS stand for: Modified Accelerated Cost Recovery System.

That is, the depreciation allowed on your early years of business use is "accelerated," whereas that allowed on its later years is switched over to straight line (depreciation). The instructions list the various property classes, and give tables of percentages for the amount of depreciation you can take.

Part III, other depreciation, is simply a summary of the current year's allowable depreciation on all prior business assets that you have placed in service. You are expected to keep a cumulative worksheet of your own, to document your entries in Part III.

Part V and its instructions define "listed property" as: (1) passenger autos, (2) pick-up trucks, (3) cellular phones, (4) computers & peripherals, (5) cameras & recorders, and (6) recreational entertainment equipment. These items are listed separately for depreciation purposes because of their propensity for personal use under the guise of business use. To make sure that you document your business use, you are asked—

Do you have evidence to support the business/investment use claimed? ☐ *Yes* ☐ *No*

If "Yes," is the evidence written? ☐ *Yes* ☐ *No.*

You are further instructed to separate your listed property assets into those used more than 50% in business, and those used 50% or less.

Part VI allows you to amortize certain specific expenditures which otherwise you would have to capitalize. The amortizable expenditures are: (a) research & experimentation, (b) forestation & reforestation, (c) business start-ups, (d) partnerships & corporate organization, and (e) exploration, mining, intangible drilling, and development efforts.

Avoid Form 6198

Schedules C, E (Part I), E (Part II: K-1's), F, and Form 4835 all have one footnote instruction in common. It appears just below the bottom line indicating net profit or net loss for the year. The instruction reads—

If a loss, you MUST check the box that describes your investment in this activity:
a. ☐ *All investment is at risk.*

b. ☐ *Some investment is not at risk.*
If you checked b, you MUST attach Form 6198.

Form 6198 is titled: ***At-Risk Limitations.*** This is an intricate and confusing form. It computes — allegedly — the amount of deductible loss you are allowed for the year. It limits your losses to your actual unrecovered real investment in the activity, where some of your indebtedness is covered by nonrecourse loans, stop-loss agreements, and seller financing arrangements. We recommend strongly that you avoid altogether the necessity of ever having to use this form.

We touched on the at-risk limitation rule (IRC Sec. 465) back in Chapter 1. In Chapter 3, we pointed out via various court rulings that any form of nonrecourse financing — where you are not personally liable for full payback — stigmatizes your activity as a sham. We want you to have no part in sham-like activities. You can avoid the stigma if you reject all variants of nonrecourse financing and put up your own money, credit, and property. If you do this, Section 465 — and Form 6198 — do not apply.

You get a tip-off to this avoidance approach in the instructions to Form 6198. In relevant part, the instructions read—

*The at-risk rules generally limit the amount of loss (including loss on the disposition of assets) you can claim to the amount that you could actually lose in the activity. . . . In most cases, you are **not** at risk for—*

* *Nonrecourse loans used to finance the activity, to acquire property used in the activity, or to acquire your interest in the activity.*

* *Cash, property, or borrowed amounts used in the activity . . . that are protected against loss by a guarantee, stop-loss agreement, or other similar arrangement.*

* *Amounts borrowed for use in the activity from a person who has an interest in the activity, other than as a creditor, or who is related to a person having such an interest.*

If you avoid all of the above not-at-risk type "investment" schemes, you can, in all clear conscience, check the MUST instruction at box a. This check-box reads, again—

a. $\boxed{\text{x}}$ *All investment is at risk.*

When you do this, no Form 6198 is required.

Form 8582: Passive Activity Losses

Although you can avoid the at-risk loss limitations of Form 6198, you cannot so readily avoid the passive activity loss rules. If, after completing Schedule E (Part I), Schedule E (Part II), or Form 4835 (farm rentals), your bottom line is a net loss, you generally have to file Form 8582: *Passive Activity Loss Limitations*. You also have to file this form if you answered "No" to the material participation question in the headportion of Schedules C and F.

The term "Passive activity" is defined in IR Code Section 469(c) as meaning—

(1) *Any activity—*
   (A) *which involves the conduct of any trade or business, and*
   (B) **in which the taxpayer does not materially participate.**
(2) *The term . . . includes any rental activity.*
(3) *The term . . . shall not include any working interest in any oil or gas property which the taxpayer holds directly or through an entity.*
(4) *Paragraphs (2) and (3) shall be applied* [irrespective of] *the taxpayer's material participation* [if any].
(5) *The term . . . includes any activity involving research or experimentation (within the meaning of section 174).*
(6) *The term . . . includes—*
   (A) *any activity in connection with a trade or business, or*
   (B) *any activity with respect to which expenses are allowable as a deduction under section 212.*
[Emphasis added.]

This statutory definition sweeps in virtually every hobby business venture that you can think of. There is some slight easing,

Form 8582	PASSIVE ACTIVITY LOSS LIMITATIONS		Year
Part I	Total Passive Activity Loss For the Year		
A	Rental real Estate With Active Participation		
1	a. Activities Net Income		
	b. Activities Net Loss		
	c. Prior Unallowed Losses		
	d. Combine Lines 1a, 1b, and 1c	▶	
B	All Other Passive Activities		
2	a. Activities Net Income		
	b. Activities Net Loss		
	c. Prior Unallowed Losses		
	d. Combine Lines 2a, 2b, and 2c	▶	
3	Combine lines 1d and 2d - then follow instructions	▶	
Part II	Special Allowance For Rental Real Estate		
Part III	Total Losses Allowed	Unallowed losses may be carried over to following years	

Fig. 5.5 - Aggregating Results from Multiple Passive Activities

however, when you "actively participate" in **rental real estate** activities. The term "active" participation means ownership of 10% or more of the activity, and you manage and oversee its operation more than 100 hours during the year. If you so qualify, then — pursuant to subsection 469(i) — you may be allowed up to $25,000 in rental property losses. To compute this *special allowance* (as it is called), you must complete Part II of Form 8582. Otherwise, your aggregate losses from all of your passive activities cannot exceed your aggregate net income from your hobby ventures. This is the gist of Section 183 (Chapter 2) all over again.

On its face, at least, Form 8582 is straightforward. Its Part I consists of two short sections, namely:

A — Rental Real Estate With Active Participation
B — All Other Passive Activities

The net income, net loss, and prior-year unallowed losses within each section are netted. Then the two sections are net-netted and entered into line 3, as presented in Figure 5.5. If line 3 results in net income or zero, all of your passive activity losses are allowed for the year. If line 3 is a net loss, then you have to follow the instructions accompanying Form 8582.

The instructions to Form 8582 comprise 12 pages and 6 worksheets, totalling about 15,000 words. The gist is that your unallowed losses for the current year may be carried over to next year . . . and to the following year . . . and so on . . . until the property is disposed of in a fully taxable transaction.

* * * * * * * * * * * * * * * * *

In the chapters which follow, we present various examples of the types of hobby businesses that we believe are tax feasible. We devote one full chapter to each of six different classes of such businesses. For all six classes, a common thread runs throughout. The activity starts as a side venture to the taxpayer's principal livelihood business. The deductions allowed are predicated upon existing tax laws . . . in concert with a bona fide profit motive.

6

ANIMAL BREEDING & SHOWING

> Successful Hobby Venturing In Animal Husbandry Requires Your Designation Of Breedstock/Sportstock — Horses Particularly — As SECTION 1231 PROPERTY. For Such Animals, All Operating Expenses PLUS A Depreciation Deduction Are Allowed. Business Animals, And The Structures, Equipment, And Vehicles That Serve Them Become COST RECOVERY ASSETS Under Section 168. Selling "Inventory Animals," Stallion Services, Mare-Boarding Services, And The Rental Of Facilities And Vehicles, Are Strong Indicators Of Your Profit Motivation. So, Too, Is The Ownership Of Animal-Associated Land.

Of all animals known to man, the horse has been his closest and most useful companion. Archaeologists estimate that the species of horse preceded the species of man by some 1,000 years or more. The first geological evidence of horse and man together appeared on chiseled stone tablets dating back to about 1400 B.C. From that time on, man and horse have been inseparable up to about the 1900's (with the advent of the automobile). As one famous historian (John T. Moore) has written: "Wherever man has left his footprint in the long ascent from barbarism to civilization, we will find the hoofprint of the horse beside it." All of the great early civilizations arose among horse-owning, horse-breeding, and horse-using nations.

Today, in the United States, it is estimated that there are approximately 4,000,000 horses in service in one form or another.

No longer are horses used in any significant way in war, agriculture, or commerce. They are used principally for sporting events, showmanship, and pleasure riding. In each of these activities there is — or can be — a bona fide profit motive. Horses can be bred, trained, raced, shown, and sold for profit-seeking ends.

The same can be said for other animals: elephants, camels, dogs, cattle, alpacas, chinchillas, and so on. In one way or another, there is profit to be made with these and other animals. To demonstrate one's profit-seeking intentions, one or more of five activities must occur, namely: (1) breeding, (2) training, (3) racing, (4) showing, and (5) selling. Obviously, those animals owned and kept as house pets, or kept elsewhere for the owner's riding, sporting, and hunting pleasure would not truly qualify as profit-seeking activities.

In this chapter, therefore, we want to focus on the ownership of animals — horses particularly — as business and investment property, rather than as personal property. We want to point out the beneficial tax features involved and the importance of Section 1231 for sale, exchanges, and involuntary conversions (disease and death) of ownership interests. We want to tell you what kind of expenses are allowed, and cite some specific examples (and experiences) with horses, alpacas, and dogs.

Animals Are "Property"

Avid animal lovers — and many who are not so avid — think of the animals they own as "almost human." We assign them names, feed and board them, groom them, pay veterinary fees, and treat them as members of our family or members of our business. This is especially true of hobby businesses where there is a strong bond between the animal and its owner. This bonding arises because animals are alive; they have emotions, intelligence, and vitality. This is unlike machinery, equipment, or vehicles used in a business.

If you look through a topical index of the Internal Revenue Code, you'll see no reference whatsoever to animals or horses. Instead, you'll find only the term *livestock* used. And, if you'll look for the tax code section that defines livestock, you'll find it in Section 1231(b)(3): ***Property Used in the Trade or Business and Involuntary Conversions***. Thus, for pure tax purposes, livestock is a form of property. It is also property of a type which is subject to "involuntary conversion" meaning: death due to disease, drought, or fatal injury.

To be more specific, Subsection 1231(b)(3) defines livestock as—

Such term includes—

*(A) cattle and horses, regardless of age, held by the taxpayer for **draft, breeding, dairy, or sporting purposes,** and held by him for 24 months or more from the date of acquisition, and*

*(B) other livestock, regardless of age, held by the taxpayer for **draft, breeding, dairy, or sporting purposes,** and held by him for 12 months or more from the date of acquisition. Such term does not include poultry.* [Emphasis added.]

It is interesting to note that subsection 1231(b)(3)(A) lumps cattle and horses together with respect to the holding period of 24 months.

The nearest other specific reference to animals is the tax code subsection 183(d), last sentence. Though we quoted this section in full in Chapter 2, the part we want to repeat here is that reference to—

*. . . the **breeding, training, showing, or racing** of horses.* [Emphasis added.]

From the above emphasized statutory phrases, we can sort out the types of livestock (animal) ownership activities which distinguish hobby businesses from livelihood business. Right off, it is obvious that any type of draft animal (for pulling or packing heavy loads) or dairy animal (for meat, milk, and dairy products) is clearly within the province of the livelihood farmer. Associated, of course, is the procreation and care of ordinary offspring for inventory and sale. Here, also, we are dealing with herds of animals: 50 head to 1,000 or more.

Hobby venturers owning livestock rarely feed and care for more than 10 to 20 animals at a time. Hobbyists are more interested in the breeding and sports use of animals with thoroughbred lines and show talent. It takes more money for these activities, too. Hobby venturers usually have the financial resources for breeding and sports use, whereas livelihood farmers often do not.

Breeding and Sporting Defined

Owning a few horses, trailering them to horse shows now and then, and riding them in annual parades is not sufficient demonstration of a hobby business venture. There has to be much more substance than this. There are two core areas of substance, namely: (a) breeding activities and (b) sporting activities. Your engagement in at least one or the other is required at all tax-significant times.

For tax purposes, the term "breeding" means more than just procreating a few new animals. It is a professional-like effort to select and acquire a superior quality species (either male or female), have the animal(s) registered, and continue the genealogy charting from prior to acquisition through records on all offspring. Some registration certification is required, together with some form of owner's membership in an established thoroughbred registering organization.

In the horse world, serious breeding intentions would be symbolized by owning one or more registered stallions (males) and/or one or more registered mares (females). The ownership need not be 100% for each horse, so long as the fractional ownership of each co-owner is clearly and expressly documented. A lineal descendant stallion or mare from a famous-named thoroughbred could easily run $100,000 to $1,000,000 in value. For such superior animals, co-ownership by two or more hobby venturers is rather common.

Also common in thoroughbred breeding circles is the owner's membership in such prestigious organizations as the American Quarter Horse Association, the Arabian Horse Club Registry of America, and the Palomino Horse Breeders of America. These and other registry organizations establish rigid standards for tracing the lines of descent and blood origins back to oriental and quasi-oriental native stock. In other cases, the tracing starts with some famous-named horse that has demonstrated very large purse winnings and/or extensive trophy winnings (**over** $1,000,000).

For tax purposes, the term "sporting purposes" involves more than just one or two grooming-type shows a year. A sporting purpose is a professional-like effort to enter your animal(s) into competitive-type activities regularly and continually throughout the year. Such activities include jockey racing, harness racing, steeplechasing, show jumping, horsemanship gaits, bareback riding, side-saddle riding, and other equestrian events where money, prizes, and trophies are awarded for win, place, and show. Included as part of such activities is the pre-event training and the post-event caring of the animal(s).

Example Expenses Allowable

For many years, the IRS has held that animal breeding and racing were two separate businesses. It treated each as a separate operation of its own, requiring that each had to pass the profit motive tests separately. The Tax Court rejected this two-business stance in *S.J. Trafficante* [60 TCM 110, TC Memo 1990-353]. The court ruled that—

Racing and breeding are regarded as part of one overall activity, given that the breeding value of a horse increased markedly if it was a good racehorse and produced offspring that fared well on the track.

As long as the breeding, training, boarding, showing, and racing is conducted with an "actual and honest objective of making a profit," the horse owner is entitled to claim full deduction for his losses. This is the common theme that comes through from over 35 documented Tax Court cases (1970-1990) where horse owners prevailed over the IRS.

For claiming the operating expenses of owning a tax-qualified horse or other animal, the use of **Schedule F**: Profit or Loss From Farming, is required. For computer identity purposes, the IRS has designated Code 270 (Animal Specialty) and Code 260 (General Livestock) as a way of distinguishing hobby farmers (Code 270) from livelihood farmers (Code 260). This "activity code" (as it is called) is entered at the very top of your Schedule F. When you enter Code 270, the IRS screening system will be looking for those expenses which clearly fall within the tax definition of breeding and sporting purposes.

To exemplify the type of expenses allowable under a Code 270 designation, Figure 6.1 is presented. Note the brief descriptive comments alongside each expense item. Some of the Figure 6.1 expense items are preprinted on Schedule F; others are not.

Those expenses listed in Figure 6.1 are those which relate strictly to the physical care and maintenance of your animal(s). There are various other (allowable) operating expenses also. There are those expenses of animal paraphernalia (saddle gear, harnesses,

Advertising	of stallion services, boarding services, sale of animals, etc.
Bedding & Supplies	other than feed and care
Boarding Fees	paid to other animal owners for feed and care
Breeding Fees	paid for stallion and bull services
Entrance Fees	for competetive events and shows
Feed Purchased	for animals, their offspring, and watchdogs
Interest	on the purchase of animals, structures, supplies, and equipment
Insurance	on animals and their safety in transit
Rent or Lease	of equipment, vehicles, land, etc.
Repairs & Maint.	to structures, equipment and vehicles used by the animals
Security	watchman, watchdogs, alarm systems, gate locks, etc.
Small Tools	used around animals, stables, and equipment
Supplies & Misc.	item of $100 or less, per unit, essential to ordinary operations
Taxes & Licences	for animals, vehicles, and equipment
Training Fees	for animal trainers and walkers
Trucking & Freight	of animals, their feed and gear
Utilities	water and power for stables & structures; debris and dung removal
Depreciation & Other Expenses (Itemize)	

Fig. 6.1 - Animal Care Expenses Allowable on Schedule F

training apparatus, grooming devices, etc.), shelter and security (barns, stables, corrals, gates, watch dogs, etc.), transportation (trucks, trailers, feeders), and taxation (licenses, permits, property taxes). There are a lot of costs associated with the care and training of competitive animals.

Breedstock, Sportstock, & Inventory

Any time an owner has a registered breeding animal in his possession, he wants to use it as such. If it is a thoroughbred stallion, he'll farm the animal out to other horse owners for stud services. He collects a fee for each impregnation of a mare (which is tax accountable income). If the breeder is a thoroughbred mare, the owner will pay stud fees to other stallion owners. Either way, there is fertilization and cross-fertilization going on all the time.

The period of gestation of a brood mare is 11 months. This means that a mare owner can only get about one foal (offspring) per animal per year. If more offspring are desired, more brood mares are required. Mares continue fertile until past age 20.

A virile stallion, on the other hand, can impregnate 35 to 50 mares per season. Normally vigorous sires can retain their potency to about age 25. Thus, a serious breeding owner would have one prime stallion and several or more brood mares.

Owning breeding animals brings up the need for classifying the offspring. In the horse world, the foals (colts if male; fillies if female) can be weaned in about two years and become fully mature in about five years. It is during this youngling stage where most of the physical/medical examinations and culling processes take place. For this culling and classification, the services of veterinarians, specialists, and consultants are required.

Most owners of brood mares try to sort their younglings into three classes, namely: Class I (new breeders), Class II (new sports type), and Class III (homebred inventory). The inventory animals (Class III), after weaning, are put up for sale to the general public. An owner may also buy other breeders' younglings (called: "purchased animals" instead of "homebred") to cull and classify as above. Those not assigned to Class I or II would be assigned Class IV (purchased inventory). After selecting the desired Class I and Class II animals for his own use, the owner may then offer his Class III and Class IV animals for sale to other professional and hobby business horse owners. Our schematic arrangement of the program involved is presented in Figure 6.2.

As a breeding owner of horses, the sale of your young animals in a systematic and ongoing way is a strong positive indicator of your profit motive. If, in addition to breeding, you train and show your retained Class II animals, and enter them into regular competition (racing, showing, trotting . . . whatever), this, too,

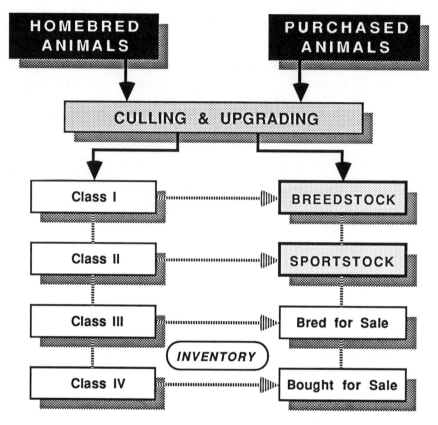

Fig. 6.2 - The Culling Process in Animal Husbandry

becomes a strong indicator of your profit motives. Of course, you need to keep good books and records of your income and winnings.

Depreciation of Breedstock/Sportstock

Once you establish some record of income, one of your Schedule F deductions against that income is a *depreciation allowance.* Animals depreciate for tax purposes, just like machinery and equipment do. The allowable rates differ but, otherwise, the depreciation principles are the same.

Section 167(a) of the tax code says very specifically that—

There shall be allowed as a depreciation deduction a reasonable allowance for the exhaustion, wear and tear . . .
(1) of property used in the trade or business, or
(2) of property held for the production of income.

Particularly note the use of the term "property." Anticipating this, we purposely stressed earlier that animals are indeed property. They, therefore, are depreciable.

Also note that there are two specific categories of property. Category (1) is that which is "used in the trade or business." In the animal world, this clearly would be your breedstock: your stallion(s) and mare(s). While being **used** for breeding purposes, your breedstock is not available for sale. It is undergoing "exhaustion, wear and tear."

Category (2) property is that which is "held for the production of income." This clearly would be your sportstock: those animals you are training for purposes of racing, showing, or trotting. While being **held** for these sporting purposes, your sportstock is not available for sale. Hence, it, too, undergoes "exhaustion, wear and tear."

For tax purposes, what do you depreciate in animals?

You depreciate the *cost basis* in each of the breedstock/sportstock animals that you own. Your cost basis is the amount of actual money, barter, and property (at fair market value) that you paid to someone to acquire an animal. Each purchase-acquired animal becomes a separate depreciable item of its own. The rationale behind depreciation is that you are allowed to recover your full purchase cost over the useful business life of each animal.

How is your cost basis determined when you breed your own animals for business, instead of acquiring them by purchase?

Answer: You have **no cost basis**! The cost of nurturing the animal while in its mother, the cost of its safe delivery, and the cost of feeding and caring for it while it matures, are allowable expenses (à la Figure 6.1) which you deduct currently as you pay them. Consequently, you have no cost basis for depreciation purposes.

When you have a purchased cost basis, when do you start taking the depreciation allowance on your tax return?

Answer: When the purchased animal is mature and "placed in service" for the business use intended. For example, if you bought a 2-year-old colt which you intend to race when it becomes a 5-year-old, your depreciation doesn't start until the animal is trained and qualified for entry into its first competitive sport. Up to this point, your expenses of training, feeding, and qualifying the animal are allowable expenses, but the recovery of your acquisition cost does not start until you register the animal for its first competition. This is the tax meaning of *when placed in service*: date, month, and year.

Statutory "Class Lives" for Depreciation

Section 168 of the revenue code is titled: Accelerated Cost Recovery System (ACRS). The ACRS idea is to enable a taxpayer to recover his purchase cost in business property in a slightly "accelerated" manner when compared to ordinary straight-line depreciation. For this purpose, certain statutory class lives have been designed. Of interest to Schedule F filers, there are six classes as follows:

3-year property; 5-year property; 7-year property; 10-year property; 15-year property; and 20-year property.

It is of interest to be informed that of the six official class lives above, only one makes any reference to animals. Horses are the only animal mentioned in all of Section 168(e)(3): Classification of Certain Property. Its subsection (A) reads—

The term "3-year property" includes—
(i) any race horse which is more than 2 years old at the time it is placed in service, and
(ii) any horse other than a race horse which is more than 12 years old at the time it is placed in service.

Apparently, the depreciation rules recognize that race horses will "wear out" long before breed and other horses will.

Other than the above subsection of 168, animal owners are left on their own as to which specific class life to use for depreciation purposes. The only help in this regard is Regulation 1.167(a)-1(b): *Useful Life*. This lengthy regulation reads in pertinent part as—

*For the purpose of section 167 [Depreciation] the estimated useful life of an asset is not necessarily the useful life inherent in the asset, but is the period over which the asset **may reasonably be expected to be useful** to the taxpayer in his trade or business or in the production of his income. This* *period shall be determined by reference to his experience with similar property taking into account present conditions and probable future developments.* [Emphasis added.]

In other words, you select a class life for each of your business animals (3, 5, 7, 10, 15, or 20 years) that is commensurate with its age and expected breeding/sporting use over time. For cost recovery purposes, your natural inclination is to select a class life that is as short as reasonable. This gives you your best depreciation allowance for each year of your hobby business activity.

Depreciation "Worksheet" Formulation

Most hobby venturers understand the tax importance of keeping good records on their business income and operating expenses. But they don't seem to understand the greater importance of capital accounting — cumulatively year after year — for the depreciable assets used in the business. This is where a *depreciation worksheet* comes in handy.

A depreciation "worksheet" is your own formulation of your **cumulative accounting** for all capital assets — depreciable and nondepreciable alike — used in the business. Cumulative accounting is required on **each asset** from its date of acquisition to its date of disposition. In other words, you need to "capital account" for your very first purchase of a business animal, and for all animals, equipment, and structures subsequent thereto, up to the date that you dispose of your last animal and cease your hobby business altogether. This is not a matter of keeping records for three to five years, then tossing them away. We are concerned with capital or cost basis records: NOT expense records. Capital accounting is an entirely different process from expense accounting.

Failure to keep, and keep current, capital records and cost basis, with cumulative depreciation adjustments as allowed, constitutes the weakest link in your profit motive attestations. Our contention is that, if you formulate and maintain good capital records, and all else fails in the IRS's profit-motive testing of you, your capital records often can pull you through. This is because, surely, one of the assets that you post will be sold someday at a gain. A capital gain upon the disposal of any asset used in business is recognized as a "profit" in the overall scheme of things.

We suggest that you prepare and organize your depreciation worksheet as outlined in Figure 6.3. Note that we present the

Part I	COLUMNAR HEADINGS
● Property item	● Depreciation method
● Cost or other basis	● Recovery class life
● Date placed in service	● Recovery rate
● Cumulative prior depreciation	● Current year depreciation

Part II	DEPRECIABLE ASSETS

☐ Breeding animals *(male, female)*

☐ Sporting animals *(age & type)*

☐ Structures *(barns, stables, fences)*

☐ Equipment *(training, riding, showing)*

☐ Vehicles *(trucks, trailers, feeders)*

Part III	NONDEPRECIABLE ASSETS

■ Land acreage *(devoted to animals)*

■ Homebred animals *(retained in business)*

■ Self-built structures *(description)*

■ Gifted property *(with no determinable basis)*

Fig. 6.3 - Organizing Your Depreciation Worksheet for Form 4562

information in three parts. The separate parts are: (1) suggested columnar headings, (2) depreciable assets, and (3) nondepreciable assets (such as land, homebred animals, self-built structures, and gifted assets).

The "suggested columnar headings" in Figure 6.3 are those which correspond closely to those officially on **Form 4562**: Depreciation and Amortization. Except for those assets placed in service during your current taxable year (which you show as a class on Form 4562), you group and summarize your total allowable depreciation on your own worksheet. You then transfer the summary amount onto Form 4562 at the line designated as—

ACRS and other depreciation (see instructions)

For other than your breedstock/sportstock animals, list your depreciable assets in descending order of class lives. That is, list the longer class lives first, and the shorter ones last. This minimizes changing your worksheet year after year. Follow with a listing of your new depreciable animals in the order of their "placement in service" dates. Also, show dates of "removal from service."

By all means, list your nondepreciable assets — those with a nonconsumable life greater than one year. Even though you get no depreciation allowance for these assets (you have no cost basis in them), your listing them helps to explain your current expenditures for feed, vet care, medicines, grooming, materials and supplies, and the like.

Be sure NOT to include your inventory animals (those bought or produced for ordinary sale) on your depreciation worksheet(s). You'll need another, less extensive, set of records for inventory.

Section 1231 Dovetailing

There is a reason why we emphasized your keeping good depreciation records. There will come a time when one or more of the assets listed on your worksheets will be sold. When this happens, they are called *asset sales*. As such, they are not considered those sales that occur in the ordinary course of your business. In a livestock business, ordinary sales are those involving the selling of inventory (animals bought for resale or those bred for sale), providing stud services, boarding services, training services, and the like.

Asset sales are more technically called: Section 1231 transactions. They are called "transactions" because they involve the disposition of business property either by sale, by exchange, or by involuntary conversion. Section 1231 is titled: *Property used in the Trade or Business and Involuntary Conversions*. It addresses the gains and losses of—

. . . any capital asset which is held more than 1 year and is held in connection with a trade or business or a transaction entered into for profit.

All Section 1231 transactions are reported on Form 4797: *Sales of Business Property*. To properly compute your gains and losses on Form 4797, you need "adjusted cost basis" information which you should have updated on your depreciation worksheets. These matters — Section 1231, Form 4797, depreciation worksheets — all tie in together when any of your assets are disposed of. Our depiction of all of this "dove tailing" is presented in Figure 6.4.

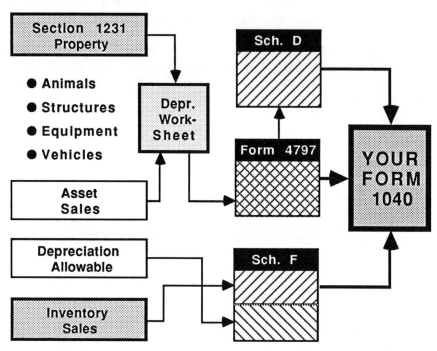

Fig. 6.4 - How Animal Breeding Details Into Form 1040

A "sale" is the outright transfer of ownership in property to another person or entity for cash and cash-equivalents. An "exchange" is the mutual transfer of "like kind" property between owners, where the owner giving up the greater equity receives cash and boot (nonlike property) so as to equalize both owners' equities at the time of the exchange. An "involuntary conversion" is the compulsory cessation of ownership caused by disease, injury, fire, storm, theft, seizure, or condemnation processes. For owners of business animals, an involuntary conversion could be one of your prize brood mares getting an infectious disease, or one of your best hurdle-jumping horses stumbling and breaking his leg and shoulder. Neither animal would be capable of resuming its breedstock/sportstock function. It would cease to have any business benefit to you and, as such, would constitute a Section 1231 "transaction."

Section 1231 is one of those "seldom known and used" tax laws that we bring to your attention. Its essence is that, if you dispose of a business-held asset at a gain, it is treated as a capital gain. If you dispose of it at a loss, it is treated as an ordinary loss. A net capital gain from Section 1231 transactions is more tax beneficial because the tax rates are usually lower than for net ordinary gains. A net ordinary loss is more tax beneficial because there is no dollar limitation to the amount of deductible loss as there is with a net capital loss (which is limited to $3,000 per year). Overall, Section 1231 gains and losses are probably the nearest you'll ever get to a "win-win" tax situation.

Clarification of "Inventory"

Most animal husbandry businesses involve breeding activities plus the buying and selling of animals for upgrading purposes. Any serious (profit-seeking) hobby venturer wants to periodically upgrade his breedstock and sportstock. This causes a lot of confusion as to what is meant by "inventory" for tax purposes. It is **not** the total of all live animals that you have on hand at the end of the year.

For tax purposes, you have two types of animals. You have Section 1231 animals, and you have inventory animals. Your Section 1231 animals are your breedstock/sportstock which is the primary thrust of your business. Ordinarily, you do not intend to sell these animals. They are property which you actually USE IN your business. As such, you receive special tax treatment on these animals when you do indeed sell, exchange, or convert them. We told you about the importance of Section 1231 above.

All other animals that you do not specifically designate as "Section 1231 property" become your inventory animals. Taxwise, they are designated: *property held for sale in the ordinary course of business.* When your inventory animals are sold, the proceeds derived are ordinary income. No special treatment of any kind applies.

When you buy animals such as horses less than two years old, they are automatically regarded as inventory. This is because they have not matured to the point where they are ready to be designated as Section 1231 property. You may sell them before they are so designated. If you buy registered animals that are mature and ready to be used in your business, you should separate and designate them as Section 1231 property. Do not lump them in with your inventory.

When you buy or breed animals with the idea of weaning, culling, and training them for sale, they are inventory. When you breed animals and are not sure what you are going to do with them, they also are inventory. The same applies to old and retireable breedstock/sportstock that have served their Section 1231 business purpose. They are inventory if you intend to sell. If you put them to death, and you have any unrecovered cost basis in those animals, you recover your unused Section 1231 costs at that time.

At the end of each year, you need to value your unsold inventory. You may do this by one of two methods: (a) farm-price method, or (b) unit-livestock-price method. The farm-price method allows you to use average competitive market values in your local area. The unit-livestock-price method requires that you segregate the animals into age groupings at one-year intervals, and then apply an average unit cost for feeding and caring for each age group. For hobby venturers, we think the farm-price method is simpler. It allows you to use the cash method of income accounting . . . which is also simpler.

Sources of Income

There is more to hobby venturing in animal husbandry than acquiring a registered breeder pair, and raking in the tax benefits. You have to "work at" the system more objectively. You have to try to produce income — at least some income — all along the way. Selling your inventory, of course, is one way. There are also other ways.

Let's suppose you have an Arabian registered stallion. You have all the papers on him, and all of his genealogy records back to at least five generations. The horse cost you $100,000 (or whatever). You have five superior brood mares of your own. Your veterinarian estimates that your stallion can live cover up to 50 mares per season, without loss of sterility. What do you do?

You hire a commercial photographer and get a full body color portrait of your stallion. Together with the photo, you make up a press release and send it to all the farming newspapers and horse-

Full Color Professional Photo

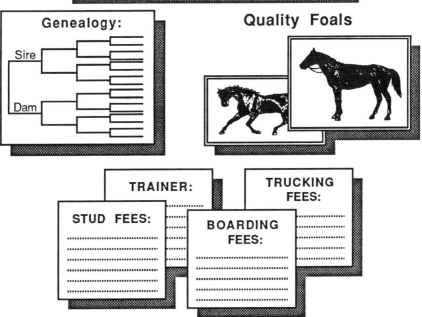

Fig. 6.5 - Illustrative Items When Advertising Animal Services

owner association newsletters in as wide an area as you can. You publicize that you have a "stallion farm" and feeding/boarding facilities. For illustration purposes, see Figure 6.5.

Then advertise in these same press release sources what you charge for stallion fees and boarding fees. Some systematic advertising program — even on a low budget — is a powerful indicator of your profit intentions. Relying on word of mouth alone is just not good enough to convince cynical tax agents.

If you have enough land acreage around, suppose you had built a training track and a show arena for your own animals. Unless you use these facilities 100% of the time, you could offer (advertise) them for rent to other animal owners. You might even sponsor training-type competitive events to get more rental use out of your facilities. Costly training/showing facilities which are unused most of the year raise questions about your profit motives.

The same questioning applies to the use of your animal transportation equipment: trucks, trailers, feeders, and the like. If they are idle too much of the year, they take on the tax character of recreational vehicles. To keep their business character alive, offer (advertise) them occasionally for use in hauling other owners' animals. Of course, you would charge some kind of trucking fee.

If you insist that your only business is that of breeding race horses for your own account, and pursue none of the income-seeking opportunities above, you **will** encounter tax difficulties. This is because it is pretty well known that—

"The pot of gold in the hills and valleys of race horse breeding is rather low-grade ore."

Our point is that horse racing alone is a long shot for demonstrating profit motive. With all of the middlemen and promotion required, you need to generate purse winnings each year greater than about five times the annual cost of feeding, caring, and depreciating the animal. This is not easy to do. Therefore, for Section 183 tax reasons, you should also pursue the mundane activities of generating income through inventory sales, stallion fees, boarding fees, rental income, and trucking fees. This **is the way** you overcome the not-for-profit presumption of Section 183(d) [two profit years out of seven for horses, and three out of five for all other animals]. See Figure 6.6 for a recap of "all of the above."

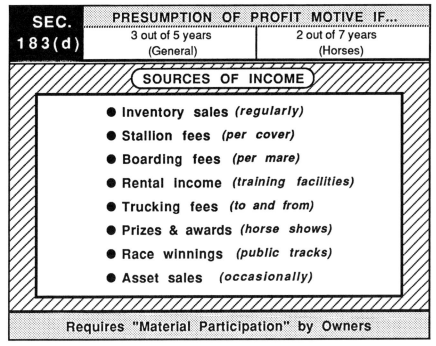

SEC. 183(d)	PRESUMPTION OF PROFIT MOTIVE IF...	
	3 out of 5 years (General)	2 out of 7 years (Horses)

SOURCES OF INCOME

- Inventory sales *(regularly)*
- Stallion fees *(per cover)*
- Boarding fees *(per mare)*
- Rental income *(training facilities)*
- Trucking fees *(to and from)*
- Prizes & awards *(horse shows)*
- Race winnings *(public tracks)*
- Asset sales *(occasionally)*

Requires "Material Participation" by Owners

Fig. 6.6 - Recap of Income Effort to Counter Not-for-Profit

Importance of Land

An additional way to overcome the not-for-profit presumption of Section 183(d) is to acquire ample land for your animal business. Every variant of animal breeding and sports requires the use of land to one extent or another. You need land for feeding and boarding; you need land for stables and corrals; you need land for mating and grazing; you need land for training and showing; and you need land as a buffer zone for neighbors and roadways.

So long as the amount of land you acquire is an integral and essential part of your animal breeding/sporting operation, it constitutes Section 1231 property. Such property, recall, is that which is USED IN the business. Without it, your animal activities would not be viable.

Yes, you could lease the land from some other farm or animal owner. But this would place more burden on the animals themselves to overcome the Section 183(d) presumption.

Furthermore, the lease payments that you make, since they would be deductible, would be construed an effort to generate tax benefits rather than profits. If you own the land, you get no equivalent-rent deduction. Therefore, the implication becomes self-evident (more or less) that you are holding the land for its appreciation in value.

The expectation of capital appreciation in a business-held asset is a good indicator of profit motivation. Even if the breeding/sporting activities of your business failed, you could still — most probably — make a profit by selling the land. But watch out for the IRS trying to separate your animal activities from your land activities, thereby asserting that you have two separate businesses.

This is what happened in the court case of *S. Thompson* [DC Conn. 90-1 USTC 50,043]. The animal business was dismal, but the sale of the land made money. The IRS wanted to separate the two and disallow all of the animal losses. The court said "No" . . . in paraphrased fashion. It held that—

> *The appreciation in the value of land upon which a horse breeding activity was conducted was properly considered* [by the taxpayer] *in determining whether the horse breeding activity was conducted with a profit motive. There was no evidence to suggest that the land was treated as anything other than an asset used, developed, and intended as a place to breed horses.*

You get our point, don't you?

Do not trust or rely on the IRS to give you proper guidance on hobby business activities involving animals. Do your own thing; but also do your earnest best to generate income and profit however you can. The three (real life) examples which follow illustrate some of the realities involved.

Example: Horse Breeding

Horse breeding, boarding, training, and showing is a perennial target for IRS audits. When a horseowner is "selected for examination," the IRS demands verification of the following:

1. **All** income sources on Schedule F
2. **All** expense deductions on Schedule F
3. **All** depreciable items on Form 4562
4. **All** transactional amounts on Form 4797

In addition, a *complete history* of the horse business is required, from startup to the present. The selectee is also required to present his/her last seven consecutive years of Schedule F activities.

In a true case recently, taxpayers with a 30-acre horse ranch were selected for audit. The husband was a security officer; the wife was a printed circuit designer. The wife was the horse business owner, and had been so for 12 consecutive years. Her Schedules F for each of the 12 years showed a net loss ranging, irregularly, from about $15,000 to $45,000 per year. By Section 183(d) standards — two profit years out of seven — she had a serious "tax problem" on her hands.

At the 3-hour audit, the wife verified *every entry* on her Schedule F, Form 4562, and Form 4797 for the selected year. She kept meticulous records. She then presented the auditor a resumé of her horse experience prior to the 12 Schedule F years. She started out as a hired stable hand, then as a training walker, then as a racehorse groomer, then as a truck driver transporting horses, until the time she bought her first registered brood mare. Her first brood mare produced 10 foals . . . which she sold.

She next presented the auditor with a complete list of 42 horses (stallions and mares) that she had bought or bartered for, in her 12 Schedule F years. She listed 53 quality foals that were produced. She listed separately the names and dates of 86 horses that she had boarded and trained for other owners. She then presented the Certificate of Registration (AQHA) of her prized stallion (Beau Brannan), the genealogy of his parents (sire: Poco Tivio; dam: Re Beau), the pedigree list of foals produced by her stallion for other brood mare owners, a sample of her Stallion Service Contract, and — finally — a full color 8-1/2" x 11" photograph of her registered stallion. That full-color photograph of a well groomed, stalwart, muscular animal was a sight to behold. The auditor treasured that photograph as though he had wished it were his own. He abruptly looked up from the photograph and said—

I have no further questions. I'll close the audit and recommend "No Change."

That was it! The audit was over. No changes whatsoever were made to any of the 12 Schedule F loss years. This is a TRUE STORY.

Example: Alpaca Breeding

Alpacas are native to the Andean highlands in South America (Bolivia, Chile, Peru) and are the smallest domestic member of the camel family. Alpacas stand about three feet high at the shoulders and about four to five feet at the head. The Inca Empire selectively bred alpacas for some 6,000 years to create the world's finest luxury fiber animal. The fleece fibers grow in eight basic colors; each fiber is a "hollow tube" which makes it a superb insulating material. The fleece sells in the U.S. for between $200 and $400 per animal, depending on fiber type: huacaya (crimped and puffy) or suri (straight and lustrous).

Peru controls as a protected species over 85% of the world's population of alpacas. The first imported alpacas to the U.S. from Chile began in 1984. Due to strict U.S. quarantine laws, a total of only about 3,500 animals have been imported (as of 1992). Most of these are in California. About 95% of the U.S. alpacas are registered with the International Llama Registry, using DNA blood typing technology.

Because of the very limited supply, alpaca breeding in the U.S. has become a unique and lucrative hobby business of its own. Registered females fetch from $12,000 to $60,000 per animal; registered males fetch from $10,000 to $35,000. The animals mature at between two and three years, and have a lifespan of 15 to 20 years.

Sensing the alpaca profit opportunities, a California taxpayer (in medical equipment sales) and his wife (a travel agent) purchased the following breedstock:

White Fawn (M)	$10,000)	
Blossom (F)	15,000)	$81,500
Catherine (F)	21,500)	
Christabel (F)	35,000)	

They also acquired about seven acres of land, and built barns, sheds, fencing, and water well system for feeding and housing their alpacas. The cost of these agricultural structures came to around $40,000.

The annual depreciation on the alpacas amounted to about $12,000; on the structures about $4,000. Veterinary fees, medicines, feed, supplies, and breeding costs run about $8,000 per year. Altogether, these alpaca breeders claimed about $25,000 in tax deductions on their 1992 Schedule F — a net loss. Their fleece income amounted to only about $500.

Like horses, the period of gestation for alpacas is about 11 months. The newborn females reach sexual maturity in about 18 months; males take about 30 months. The alpaca fleece is harvested every 12 to 18 months.

Because alpacas are "new kids on the block" in tax administration circles, it will be interesting to see how the IRS interprets Section 183(d). Will it accept 2-(profit years)-out-of-7 as for horses, or will it insist on 3-out-of-5 as for other animals? The fact that there is such a shortage of alpacas compared to horses (about one alpaca for every 1,000 horses) should, in and of itself, be the real profit motivator.

Example: Dog Racing

In the U.S., dogs are generally thought of as house pets. Yes, there are guard dogs, seeing-eye dogs, sniffer dogs (for drug enforcement), police dogs, hunting dogs, and so on. But, by and large, there are rather limited hobby venture opportunities with dogs. Of the more than 100 different breeds, only one — the greyhound — has shown any significant potential for profit making. That potential lies strictly in racing . . . and pari-mutuel betting.

Greyhound racing was first introduced in the U.S. around 1910. This was an outgrowth of the hunting of game with fast hounds. Greyhounds chase their prey by sight rather than by smell. This characteristic, together with their slender bodies, long legs, and deep chests, enable them to run at speeds up to 50 mph. In the racing mode, except for size differences, the physical silhouettes of greyhounds and racehorses are much the same. This explains why, in the early years, idle racehorse tracks were used for greyhound dog racing. An electrically controlled mechanical hare was used as a lure.

In 1925, the first dog-only racetrack was opened in St. Petersburg, Florida. Since that time, some 19 states (Arizona and Florida, primarily) have legalized greyhound racing. Although the sport was first developed in California, it is illegal in that state.

For entry into qualified races, a greyhound must be at least 12 months old. Each racedog is inspected and certified by a licensed veterinarian. Th dogs race around a 3/8-mile track in less than one minute's time. A superior dog will race about twice a week. A grueling, culling, and grading process is based on each dog's record in previous races. For well bred and well trained animals, their racing career averages about one year; in rare cases, two years.

The short racing career of greyhounds creates a tax dilemma for their owners. As Section 1231 animals, the shortest depreciation class life is three years. This is the same as that for racehorses, two years or older. The IRS won't budge on allowing a class life less than three years. For an animal whose productive racing life is 12 to 18 months, what does an owner do with his "wornout" greyhounds?

Answer: He shoots them! Yes, this is true. An owner is forced to do this for tax reasons.

Approximately 50,000 greyhound racing dogs are put to death each year, by shooting. Most are shot at about age 2, and certainly by age 3. When a wornout racing dog is shot, the owner's unrecovered cost in that dog is deductible in full at that time. Otherwise, an owner has to carry his unrecovered costs on his tax books until the animals can be sold (there is no market for race-exhausted greyhounds) or they die naturally.

Shooting a racedog at age two or three when his normal lifespan would be 10 to 15 years is clearly inhumane. But this is the reality of Tax Life, USA . . . and of Section 183(d).

7

FARMS, ORCHARDS, VINEYARDS

When Acquiring Agricultural Land, It Should Be Appraised For Its "Highest And Best Use" Some 10 To 20 Years Away. This Is A Key Factor In Establishing Profit Motive In Your Hobby Farm, Orchard, Or Vineyard. Important, Too, Is Refusal Of Government "Assistance" (Subsidies) And Avoidance Of Farming Syndicates. Subsidies Limit Your Control And Use Of Land; Syndicates Limit Your Allowable Expense Deductions. Because Agricultural Crops Are Seasonal, Full-Time Participation Is Not Required. What Is Required, However (For Tax Reasons), Is That You Become A Member In The FARM COOPERATIVE Where You Consign Your Crops For "Collective Marketing."

For hobby business purposes, there are three attractive features to investing in farms, orchards, and vineyards. The first and foremost is that the common underlying asset is land. The acquisition and ownership of land is real; the land is there whether you work its crops or not. There is only a finite amount of land on earth. If it happens to be in the right location, there is a long-term profit potential in appreciation of the land alone.

The second hobby business feature of farms, orchards, and vineyards is that its crops are seasonal. Usually, there is only one harvest season for the year. This means that as a hobby venturer, your physical presence is not required continuously, all year long. If you appear on the scene during the critical periods of planting and harvest, you can readily qualify as an active (over 100 hours) or material (over 500 hours) participant. This means that you can take long weekends and/or long vacations from your livelihood business to "run the farm." During your absence from the land, you can engage a resident manager or caretaker, if conditions warrant.

The third attractive feature is that farming operations require a significant amount of nonpassenger-carrying equipment. In other words, farm equipment does not carry with it the tax stigma of passenger autos, recreational vehicles (boats, trailers, airplanes), and sporting activities (motorcycle racing, sky diving, water skiing, etc.). Farm equipment qualifies as 100% nonpersonal-use property. It, therefore, enjoys the full benefits of applicable investment credits, accelerated depreciation, expense elections, and repairs and maintenance.

Thus, in this chapter we want to focus on those kinds of hobby farming, orcharding, and vineyarding that have proven to be tax successful. In the process, we will define the types of activities to stay away from . . . and why. We'll also cite the ownership and management style of three actual taxpayers — a mechanical engineer, an airline pilot, and a school teacher — who have carried on their activities successfully. In all three cases, the end goal was a full-fledged occupation after retiring from their livelihood businesses.

Specialize Your Crop

For hobby business purposes, a "farm" is a flat area of agricultural land on which surface and root crops are grown. An "orchard" is a foothills and gentle sloping area of land where fruit and nut trees prosper. A "vineyard" is a hilltop or series of hilltop areas on the hillsides of which grape vines and other stake-type berry vines grow. Each of these three topographic land forms offers different potentials for long-term profit. We'll explain these differences later.

Before any long-term profits can arise, one has to "employ the land" in an intelligent manner. This is necessary in order to take your tax deductions legitimately, year after year. For hobby venturers, the best way to do this is to specialize in the crop or crop types that you grow. Preferably, select one basic crop type, with no more than three variant species of that type. For example, if you have a citrus orchard, you could grow oranges, lemons, and limes simultaneously. Or, if you have an almond orchard, you could have different rows of walnut and almond trees. By having two or three different species of a selected crop type, you spread your risks in the event of drought, disease, freezes, and market fluctuations. Crop specialization and risk management are good indicators of your inner motivations towards profit.

By specializing in one crop type, you can become quite expert on your own. You might contact an agricultural consultant to get you going. But, thereafter, you can research the market place, the requisite soil preparations, the treatment for drought and disease, and the harvesting and storage requirements of that one crop type. You can specialize without jeopardizing your livelihood business, much as any hobbyist would do after hours, on weekends, or on vacations. There is little or no conflict of time.

By being an active specialist in one crop type, you are less apt to be tax hassled as a pure passive entrepreneur. You join whatever farm cooperative or commodity group that shares knowledge in your selected crop. As you become more expert in that crop type, you gradually improve your operations towards the premium end of the commodity line. You focus more and more on the premium-only markets. Because of the uncontrollable risks of nature, livelihood farmers cannot afford this as readily as can hobby farmers. Hobby farmers can take more risks because they have other sources of income, whereas livelihood farmers do not.

You Own the Land

The IRS has come up with a hobby business classification called "limited entrepreneur." This is a passive investor who has no direct investment in the agricultural land on which he produces crops. He and his associates, who are also passive investors, hire a manager to run things by leasing cheap available land. Some speculative, exotic-sounding crop is proposed. There is no existing market for the crop. Consequently, the operation requires extensive land-development expenditures and plantings, for which significant upfront tax deductions may accrue. This type of farming operation is clearly a not-for-profit endeavor.

To thwart the IRS's attempt to classify you as a limited entrepreneur, you — with one or more close family members — must own the land. This means that you must acquire the land in your own name under the best financial terms that you can arrange. You can hold title in any form that you want: joint tenancy, tenants in common, partnership, trust, S corporation, or whatever. It is not so much the title form as it is the fact that you are the sole owner or co-owner of the land. Direct ownership of land gives you control over the access and use of that land.

Being the owner of agricultural land, you have an investment at stake which, in almost every case, will exceed your annual deductible expenses. This is true whether you use the land as a farm, orchard, or vineyard.

To emphasize that your venture is bona fide, before its acquisition you investigate the land thoroughly. You get a chemical analysis of its soil, a few core samples for water and minerals, a topographic survey, a weather and climate analysis, and a general roadmap of the surrounding area. You investigate the land from the point of view of its *highest and best use* some 10 to 20 years down the line. For this, you'll need an appraiser and a consultant who provide you with written reports and recommendations.

For example, suppose you want to acquire 100 acres of land: either farm, orchard, or vineyard. If you intend to surface crop it, have the site appraised for its potential light industry or multiple housing development. Flat land accessible to urban growth areas offers this potential. If tree cropping is your choice, have the land appraised for its potential use as professional offices or fine homes. Orchard settings with mature trees — only a few of which are removed for construction purposes — are ideal settings on the outskirts of suburban areas. If vineyard cropping is your choice, have the hilltop appraised as view property for expensive homesites and social clubhouses. There is something prestigious about a small vineyard and winery adjacent to hill home property.

If you have your intended agricultural land acquisition surveyed and appraised for its future sale potential, your underlying profit motive stands strong and tall. Of course, the IRS will still hassle you if you don't make a profit during each intermediate year. But you do have a third-party document to back up your long-term intentions. Although it tries, it is difficult for the IRS to totally disregard a professional "highest and best use" appraisal of your land. In Figure 7.1, we present the general idea behind your agricultural land intentions.

Resist Government "Assistance"

There was a time in the history of mankind where some ruling sovereign owned (by force) all accessible land that his warriors could control. Land wars and territorial wars were fought over this sovereign power concept. Today, as a result of many popular

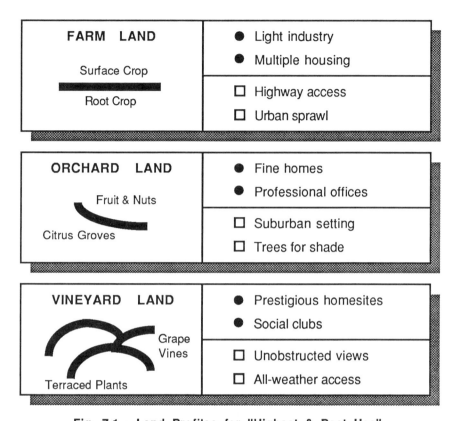

Fig. 7.1 - Land Profiles for "Highest & Best Use"

uprisings and revolutions, the concept of private ownership of land has emerged. This concept is particularly strong in the United States. Even so, not all land in the U.S. is privately owned. The great bulk is still owned by various federal, state, and local governing agencies. What government doesn't own, it tries to control through carrot-like "assistance" programs.

At the federal level, there is a whole litany of agricultural subsidy programs designed to provide financial assistance to farmers and ranchers. In the IR Code, the recipients of this government money are designated as holding "Section 126 property." Officially, Section 126 is titled: *Certain Cost-Sharing Payments*. This section lists 10 or so government programs for soil and water conservation, agriculture conservation, land clearing, land banking (keeping land out of usual production), protecting the environment, and other politically-appealing causes.

Most of the federal subsidy programs are directed at livelihood farmers and ranchers who own vast acreages of land. In the right agricultural areas, hobby farmers could also qualify for subsidy assistance. However, we strongly recommend that you **not** participate in any federal subsidy (payments) program. If you do participate voluntarily, the IRS will construe your participation as self-negation of your long-term profit motives.

At the state level, property tax relief incentives are offered for dedicating all or portions of your land to "open space," coastal access, protecting the environment, and other public easements. Again, as a hobby venturer, we urge that you not participate in these enticements. As tempting as it is to accept some property tax relief, it ties your hands and limits your control over the timing of the disposition (by sale or exchange) of your land.

At the local level, you are offered variances from zoning ordinances and some easing of restrictions on operating permits, if you dedicate some portion of your property as a public easement. Most easements are for purposes of using your land for utility lines (such as cable TV), fire and water mains, erosion control, road widening, and other public accesses. All forms of easements restrict the use of your land and detract from its "highest and best use" value, when the land is someday sold.

If you accept so much as $1 in any form of government assistance, you have surrendered a substantial amount of personal control over your land.

During your absence from your land, you may need some extra surveillance and protection from the local fire, police, and sheriff's departments. If so, try to enter into a private contract for these services. Go out of your way to make sure that you pay the respective government agencies for the extras rendered. This should ward off any implications of your engaging in illegal practices with local officials. A taxpayer/landowner engaging in illegal practices (bribes, kickbacks, hush payments, etc.) is a dead giveaway to the IRS that he is not in the venture for long-term profit purposes.

Avoid Farming Syndicates

A "farming syndicate" carries with it an adverse tax stigma. It is IRS classified as a tax shelter likely to be engaged in sham transactions. Because of this classification, farm-type expense deductions are severely limited. The limitations are set forth in tax code Section 464: *Limitations on Deductions for Certain Farming Expenses.* Here, the term "farming" means—

> *. . . the cultivation of land or the harvesting of **any** agricultural commodity.*

This includes orchards and vineyards.

Section 464 targets two types of taxpayers, namely:

1. Those associated with farming syndicates (as defined below), and
2. Those persons prepaying 50 percent or more of certain farming expenses [Sec. 464(f)].

The idea behind Section 464 is to require that "economic substance" be performed before any expenses for *feed, seed, fertilizer, and other similar farm supplies* are allowed. Recall our discussion in Chapter 1, Figure 1.1, regarding economic performance.

A farming syndicate is defined in Section 464(c) as a partnership or any other enterprise (association, trust, or S corporation) engaged in farming if—

(a) any ownership interests are required to be registered with any federal or state agency regulating security sales, or

(b) more than 35 percent of the losses incurred during any period are allocable to limited partners or limited entrepreneurs.

A limited partner is one whose loss liability in the venture is limited to the dollar amount that he has actually invested. A limited entrepreneur is one whose loss liability may exceed his investment, but who takes no active role in farm management.

If you and/or close members of your family own and control the land, as we have urged above, Section 464 does not apply. Subsection 464(c)(2) specifically **excludes** "holdings attributable to active management" from the general limitations of Section 464(a). Not excluded, however, are those landowners who have "excess prepaid farm supplies for the taxable year." This is the 50 percent prepayment rule that we should tell you more about. It purposely targets hobby farmers who do not live on the land to work it as their principal business activity.

The 50% Rule: Prepaid Expenses

Subsection 464(f)(1): *Certain Persons Prepaying 50 Percent or More of Certain Farming Expenses*, reads in full as—

> *In the case of a taxpayer to whom this subsection applies, subsections (a) and (b) shall apply to the excess of prepaid farm supplies of such taxpayer in the same manner as if such were a farming syndicate.*

Subsections (a) and (b) limit the deductibility of amounts prepaid for "feed, seed, fertilizer, or other similar farm supplies" to those amounts **actually used or consumed** in the taxable year for which the deductions are allowed.

In other words, a hobby business farmer (the taxpayer for whom subsection (f) applies) is treated as a member of a farming syndicate if he prepays more than 50% of the total deductible farming expenses for the year. The term "deductible farming expenses" means—

> *. . . any amount allowable as a deduction (including any amount allowable as a deduction for depreciation or amortization) which is properly allocable to the trade or business of farming* [Sec. 464(f)(4)(C)].

Subsection 464(f)(1) — the 50% rule — applies only to the **excess** over 50% of the prepaid supplies. To avoid this rule, one voluntarily limits his prepaid supplies to 50% or less of those actually consumed. A useful yardstick for voluntarily holding back on your prepaid supplies is to use the aggregate average of all deductible expenses for the preceding three years. By prepaying for supplies not more than 50% of these expenses, a hobby farmer can take a tax deduction for them in the year paid, instead of waiting for the year that the supplies are actually consumed. Prepaying of certain expenses can be particularly tax beneficial in good harvest years. We have tried to clarify this 50% rule by our depiction in Figure 7.2.

Subsection 464(d) grants an exception to the 50% rule if the excess unconsumed supplies on hand at the close of the taxable year are on account of: "fire, storm, disease, drought, or other casualty." Subsection 464(f)(3)(A)(ii) grants a further exception where there

CURRENT PAYMENTS	PREPAYMENTS FUTURE CONSUMPTION	
Supplies Actually Consumed During the Taxable Year Fully Allowed	Up to 50% Prepayment Allowed	Excess Over 50% SUSPENDED Until Supplies Actually Consumed

Fig. 7.2 - The 50% Rule on Prepaid Farm Supplies

are excess prepaid farm supplies on hand by reason of "any change in business operation directly attributable to extraordinary circumstances."

If you are going to be a hobby business farmer (orchardist, wine grower) for the long term, we see no point in prepaying for supplies except in good harvest years. Otherwise, you get caught up in the cycle of prepaying (for unused supplies) year after year, just for the tax benefits. It becomes wasteful and indicative of poor management, when you accumulate an overabundance of these supplies.

Preparatory & Preproduction Expenses

There is a continual war going on between the IRS and agricultural landowners. The IRS wants to capitalize every expenditure before crops are produced and harvested. The landowner wants to expense these items when he incurs them. If the landowner is a hobby farmer instead of a livelihood farmer, the IRS will insist that the not-for-profit rules of Section 183 apply, and that its capitalization dictates apply. This whole affair has been an ongoing squabble since the IRS ascended to power in 1913.

Having said the above, here's the situation as we see it. In any farming operation, there are four chronological stages of activity. Once the land is acquired, the operational stages are:

1. The preparatory stage.
   — the clearing, leveling, grading, ditching, and contouring of the land for the crop intended.
2. The preproductive stage.
   — the conditioning of the soil and the planting of plants, trees, and vines and nurturing of them until they begin blossoming.
3. The production stage.
   — the nurturing and servicing of the plants, trees, and vines from the time of blossoming to the time of fruition and harvesting.
4. The storage stage.
   — the removal and transport of the crops from the land to storage (and carrying as inventory) until they can be sold or otherwise disposed of.

We depict these four stages in Figure 7.3 and indicate the general tax rules that apply.

In most cases, expenditures incurred during the preparatory period of establishing a farm, orchard, or vineyard must be capitalized. That is, the preparatory costs are **added** to the acquisition cost of the land. Such costs include the planting of noncrop trees (shade, ornamental, boundary), well drilling, clearing brush, leveling land, laying pipes, installing drain tiles or ditches, constructing tanks or reservoirs, constructing dams, or building roads and other machinery accesses. There are two exceptions to this general capitalization rule which we'll mention shortly below.

Preproduction or development costs also, generally, must be capitalized. These are those amounts expended in the development of farms, orchards, and vineyards before reaching the productive state of the first commercial crop. A "preproduction period" is construed to mean *more than two years* from the initial planting to the first crop. Such costs include the nursery stock, plant stakings, spraying, irrigation, fertilizing, pruning, grafting, removing dead plantings, and so on. These can be amortized over the commercial lifespan of the crops produced.

In lieu of capitalizing the preparatory costs and/or amortizing the preproduction costs, one may exercise an election not to have the capitalization rules apply. Subsection 263A(d)(3): *Election; Exception for Farming Businesses*, paragraph (A) says—

ACQUISITION OF THE LAND

1. THE PREPARATORY STAGE
- ☐ Capital costs: add to value of land

2. THE PREPRODUCTION STAGE
- ☐ Capital expenditures: amortize over useful life

3. THE PRODUCTION STAGE
- ☐ Expenses currently deductible: for servicing and harvesting

4. THE STORAGE STAGE
- ☐ Freight-in: adds to inventory value; storage rent is expensed

DISPOSITION OF THE LAND

Fig. 7.3 - The Operational Stages of Any Farming Business

If a taxpayer makes an election under this paragraph, this section [263A: Capitalization of Certain Expenses] shall not apply to any plant produced in any farming business carried on by the taxpayer.

This is the first exception to the general capitalization rule.

The second exception to the general capitalization rule has to do with soil and water conservation expenditures. This exception, however, is applicable only after a farm, orchard, or vineyard is in its productive state generating some gross income. Section 175: *Soil and Water Conservation Expenditures*, addresses this point. If the expenditures are made in accordance with an approved plan by a federal or state agency, then up to "25 percent of the gross income derived from farming" may be expensed rather than capitalized. If no income is generated, Section 175 is beneficially moot.

Productive Stage Expenses

Once a farming operation reaches the crop productive stage, the general capitalization rules do not apply. Since the landowner derives business-type income, all of his production-related expenses are deductible. They are deductible even if they produce a net operating loss for the taxable year.

Regulation 1.162-12(a): *Expenses of Farms Engaged in For Profit*, states in pertinent part that—

*A farmer who operates a farm for profit is entitled to deduct from gross income as necessary expenses **all amounts actually expended** in carrying on the business. The cost of ordinary tools of short life or small cost, such as hand tools (shovels, rakes, etc.) may be deducted. . . . The cost of seeds and young plants which are purchased for further development and cultivation prior to sale in later years may be deducted as an expense for the year of purchase provided the farmer follows a **consistent practice** of deducting such costs as an expense from year to year. . . .[Emphasis added.]*

Section 180: *Expenditures by Farmers for Fertilizer, Etc.*, continues the above theme by stating—

A taxpayer engaged in the business of farming may elect to treat as expenses which are not chargeable to capital account expenditures (otherwise chargeable to capital account) which are paid or incurred by him during the taxable year for the purchase or acquisition of fertilizer, lime, ground limestone, marl, or other materials to enrich, neutralize, or condition land used in farming, or for the application of such materials to such land. The expenditures so treated shall be allowed as a deduction.

Based on the above, a representative list of the types of operating expenses that are tax deductible is presented in Figure 7.4. In one arrangement or another, many of the Figure 7.4 expenses are preprinted on Schedule F (Farm Income and Expenses) and Form 4835 (Farm Rental Income and Expenses). When entering any operational expenses on Schedule F or Form 4835, care is required NOT to deduct the farmowner's labor, that of his spouse, or that of his children. The same precaution (nondeductibility) applies to

Schedule F	FARM INCOME AND EXPENSES
Form 4835	FARM RENTAL INCOME AND EXPENSES

IMPORTANT NOTE: All expenses must relate directly to farm products, services, machinery, or buildings.

1.	Advertising	13.	Insurance
2.	Amortization	14.	Interest paid
3.	Auto & truck	15.	Labor hired
4.	Board & room	16.	Machine hire
5.	Breeding fees	17.	Rent or lease
6.	Chemicals (spray)	18.	Repairs & maintenance
7.	Conservation	19.	Seed & plants
8.	Depreciation	20.	Storage & warehousing
9.	Feed purchased	21.	Supplies & small tools
10.	Fertilizers & lime	22.	Taxes (property)
11.	Freight & trucking	23.	Utilities
12.	Gas, fuel, & oil	24.	Vet fees & medecines
	Other: itemize		Other: itemize

Listed Alphabetically: Most (not all) are preprinted on applicable tax forms.

Fig. 7.4 - Gamut of Expenses Allowable on Sch. F and Form 4835

food, supplies, utilities, repairs, and vehicles used by the landowner and his family.

The cost of farm machinery, equipment, farm buildings, and storage sheds represents a capital investment. Such costs are not deductible as an expense except to the extent of the annual depreciation allowed.

Kansas Farm: California Owner

Let us now exemplify how hobby farming can work. The taxpayer was a mechanical engineer (real case) who lived in California and owned a farm in Kansas. He owned some 1,600 acres of prime land in the wheat belt of that state. He acquired the land by inheritance from his parents, who inherited it from his grandparents.

Instead of working the land himself, the owner visited the Kansas farm site, advertised for a sharecropper, and entered into a sharecropping agreement with a livelihood wheat farmer. The sharecrop farmer had all of his own equipment and machinery except for an $80,000 wheat harvesting combine which he needed. The California owner purchased the combine on contract. The combine was used on the owner's Kansas farm, and, when not in use there, was rented to other wheat farmers in Kansas. The landowner and sharecropper both joined (by purchasing stock in) the local County Farmers Association: a duly incorporated cooperative.

At planting time, the California owner would take a week's vacation from his livelihood job. He would fly to Kansas and, together which his sharecropper, would arrange for the preparation of the land and the purchase of seed and fertilizer. At harvest time, he would take three weeks' vacation and, together with his adult son, would go to work on the Kansas farm. The owner would oversee the harvesting, help operate the combine, supervise the loading (and the cropsharing), and transport his share of the crop proceeds to the farm cooperative granary.

At income tax filing time, the California owner prepared Form 4835: Farm Rental Income and Expenses. He reported his proper share of the crop proceeds (typically 35%) and of the crop supplies and maintenance expenses. He also deducted all nonshared ownership expenses, such as property taxes, utilities, farm maintenance, his business trips to Kansas (from California), and his temporary living expenses (food, motel, and phone) while there at planting and harvest times. He also reported the combine rental income and claimed all allowable depreciation (on Form 4562), repairs, and fuel for the combine machine.

Since he produced a wheat crop in Kansas while living in California, he had to file a Kansas nonresident tax return. He also had to file a California resident tax return reporting the Kansas net income or loss. California taxes out-of-state income to its residents, but allows an *other state credit* for a **portion** (not all) of the tax paid to the other state. As usual with any farming operation, there were good years (net profit) and bad years (net loss).

Fruit Orchard: Retirement Site

Let us also exemplify how hobby orcharding can work. The taxpayer was an airline pilot (real case) who lived in a metropolitan area (accessible to his flight center) and bought a 50-acre orchard in the distant foothills. The orchard was located about 135 miles from his primary residence. The pilot planned to retire there one day.

The orchard was fully developed with mature apple, peach, and pear trees, but was in need of substantial restorations and replantings. The prior owner (a livelihood orchardist) had become disabled and needed to sell. After having the trees examined by a horticultural specialist, the pilot owner set about removing dead and diseased trees and replacing them with young fruit-bearing trees. He retilled the soil, replenished the nutrients, put in a new irrigation and drainage system, and put up new fences as needed. He repaired the old farmhouse, barns, sheds, gates, and wells. The pilot (and his family) referred to the old farmhouse as his "working vacation" cottage. Airline pilots are typically on-duty for two weeks and off-duty two weeks (each month).

The pilot (plus his wife, and children when out of school) did most of the physical work himself. He bought (on contract) new tractors, fruit trailers, and new sorting, drying, packing, and refrigeration equipment. He also bought the prior owner's stock shares in the local farm cooperative. He contracted out to other orchardists the routine chores of weed control, tree trimming, fruit picking, and raking/removing of dropped fruit on the ground. He engaged local labor for the fruit shed sorting and packing. He stored his premium crop in his own walk-in commercial refrigerator, and transported his regular crop to the farm cooperative. He sold what premium crop he could to independent produce buyers (when the price was right) and consigned the remainder to the cooperative.

At income tax filing time, he prepared Schedule F (Farm Income and Expenses) and Form 4562 (Depreciation and Amortization) for his orchard business. Because the orchard had been run down for some years, he reported a net loss for several years in a row. Because of these losses, he scrupulously avoided claiming any of his "vacation cottage" expenses on Schedule F. He intended ultimately to demolish the old farmhouse and build a much larger modern home when he retired. Upon retirement, he intended to become a full-time orchardist.

Grape Vineyard: Prenuptial Land

Let us further exemplify how hobby vineyarding can work. The taxpayer was a school teacher (real case) who married and bought an older home on a barren hillside. When his first child was born, the taxpayer's father bought some 15 acres of surrounding hilltop/hillside land and gifted it to his son. The father had the land agriculturally and horticulturally appraised for its vineyard potential. Three different species of grapes were recommended, one for each of three different topographic and sun exposure areas. The father had invested in wineries and vineyards before, and was encouraging his son to try his hand at vineyarding. Teachers, generally, have more holidays and longer summer vacations than most other livelihood occupations.

Tragedy struck. The teacher's wife died while giving birth to his second child. As a result, the vineyard idea lay dormant for several years. When the teacher remarried, he made a prenuptial agreement with his new wife and partitioned the intended vineyard land as his sole and separate property.

After remarrying, the taxpayer had his partitioned land disked, contoured, terraced, and furrowed. By means of light truck accesses and pathways, he divided the vineyard area into three separate fields. He measured the distances between the intended vine plantings, dug the holes, installed stakes, and strung wire (horizontally) for growth control. He also installed an overhead sprinkler system which was hooked up to the local water company. Most of this preparatory work was done by the taxpayer himself, assisted by his father and brother on occasion. He bought vine starters from a farm nursery and had contract labor do the plantings (one field at a time). It took about three years before the vines reached their first marketable crop stage.

For the first crop harvesting, the taxpayer rented (from another vineyard owner) picking, sorting, and hauling equipment. He located an unprocessed-grape wholesaler to whom he sold his first crop. He soon realized that he could have gotten a better price deal had he bought into the local farm cooperative . . . which he subsequently did. He also started buying his own harvesting and servicing equipment, and instituted a systematic replanting program of replacing poor and undernourished vines. He was trying to upgrade his crop for better price potential. Unfortunately, he encountered a 5-year drought spell during which period his irrigation water was rationed.

At income tax time, the taxpayer/teacher/vineyardist filed his Form 1040 as *married separate.* He attached Schedule F and Form 4562 (depreciation, etc.). He capitalized (via depreciation and amortization) his preparatory costs and initial plantings, but expensed all harvesting and replanting expenditures. He depreciated his few farm structures, vehicles, and equipment as appropriate. Because of the long drought, his crops were poor in yield and quality. Consequently, his Schedule F showed a substantial net loss for more than five years in a row. These losses offset most of his teacher's salary. This resulted in a refund of his entire W-2 income tax withholdings (for those years). By contrast, his wife (a nurse) got no corresponding refunds whatsoever.

Farm Cooperatives

In all three examples above, land ownership was the initial factor in establishing that the hobby ventures were bona fide. Equally important, was each owner's active and material participation in working the land (farm, orchard, or vineyard). Yet, another key factor was each owner's membership in a local farm cooperative. Because of the "collective marketing" aspects of these cooperatives, participants generally get a better price deal for their crop than by selling wholesale individually.

When properly organized and managed, farmers' cooperatives are tax exempt entities pursuant to Section 521 of the Internal Revenue Code. This section is titled: *Exemption of Farmers' Cooperatives From Tax.* It describes these exempt entities as—

> *Farmers', fruit growers', or like associations organized and operated on a cooperative basis—*
> *(A) for the purpose of **marketing the products** of members or other producers, and turning back to them the proceeds of sales, less the necessary marketing expenses, on the basis of either the quantity or the value of the products furnished by them, or*
> *(B) for the purpose of **purchasing supplies and equipment** for the use of members or other persons, and turning over such supplies and equipment to them at actual cost, plus necessary expenses.* [Emphasis added.]

For running the cooperative venture, capital stock is typically required. This means that the members of the cooperative contribute operating capital (via the purchase of stock) and become part owners (patrons) thereof. The tax exempt status of the cooperative hinges on the concept that all net earnings of the cooperative, if any, are passed through to its patrons in the form of dividend distributions. These "patronage dividends" (as they are called) are taxable to the individual members rather than at the cooperative level.

Established cooperatives rarely pay their members cash for the crops consigned to them for marketing. Instead, they "pay" in the form of *per-unit retain certificates* (or allocations). Each certificate cites a specified dollar amount per unit of product, times the number of units to be marketed for the member. These certificates (allocations) become agricultural script which are as useful as money. They can be "sold" to other members or to nonmembers, or they can be exchanged for the purchase of supplies and equipment from the cooperative. They also can be surrendered to accepting nonmember farm suppliers and equipment brokers.

At the end of the year, the cooperative issues to each member patron Form 1099-PATR: *Taxable Distributions Received From Cooperatives*. The purpose of this tax form, of course, is to remind each recipient member to include his patronage dividends AND his per-unit retains in the gross income portion of his Schedule F and/or Form 4835. For this purpose, there is a special income entry on Schedule F and on Form 4835. This line officially reads—

Total cooperative distributions [Form(s) 1099-PATR]

Our contention is that membership in a farm cooperative is prima facie evidence of your profit motive. If you have a bona fide entry on the PATR income line of your Schedule F or Form 4835, it is difficult for the IRS to assert arbitrarily that your hobby business (farm, orchard, or vineyard) is primarily for pleasure and recreation.

8

VACATION PROPERTY RENTALS

If You Answer "No" To The 14-Day 10%-Rental Question On Schedule E (1040), The Vacation Nature Of Your Property Is Temporarily Disregarded. This Enables You To Show A Net Loss For At Least 2 Out of 5 Consecutive Years. To Be Allowed This Loss, However, Your Deductible Expenses Must Be ATTRIBUTABLE TO The RATIO Of Fair Rental Days To Your Total Use Days (Personal, Below Market, And Fair Rental). Section 280A: Rental Of Vacation Homes, Etc., Requires Coordination With Section 183. All Vacation Property Should Be Acquired With One Of Two Preplanned SELLING Strategies In Mind.

With vacation property, many owners engage in hobby business activities without realizing that they are doing so. They engage in "business" the moment they rent their property to others and collect money — or barter — therewith. Whether they rent to family, friends, or strangers, it makes no difference. If the amount of rent or rent equivalent is "fair and competitive" in the general area where the property is used, the owners are in the vacation rental business.

Taxpayers buy vacation property primarily for their own recreation and pleasure. Vacation times are those periods of rest and freedom from one's livelihood work. As such, vacation times are short in length when compared to a 365-day ownership year. Consequently, an owner of vacation property has many vacant days where he could offer the property for use by others.

For our purposes, "vacation property" is any form of temporary dwelling unit or recreational vehicle capable of accommodating two or more persons at one time. Included are such items as a cabin in the mountains, a cottage near the seashore, a condo in a ski area, a small country inn (bed and breakfast), a motor home, a camper-trailer, an off-road vehicle (nonfarm), a dune buggy, a private aircraft, a pleasure boat (cabin cruiser, yacht, sail, motor), and so on. In other words, vacation property is of a type and at a location where a family of two or more persons would spend one, two, or three weeks of the year vacationing, pure and simple There is no pretense that the property is being used otherwise.

In the tax world, special *vacation rental rules* apply. These rules essentially say that you must allocate all expenses and depreciation in direct proportion to the number of days that the property is actually rented at fair market value during the year. In certain cases, the rules provide that your directly allocable expenses cannot exceed your fair rental income. In other cases, if you can show some "incidents" of the profit motive, you can claim a net loss . . . for a limited time. These and other vacation property rules are the focus and thrust of this chapter.

General Disallowance Rules

Vacation property sends a telegraphic message to the world that it is personal use property. It may be temporarily used for other purposes, but it was acquired primarily for the pleasure and convenience of the owner. Consequently, it should come as no surprise that general disallowance tax rules apply.

Actually, there are two such rules, namely: Sections 262 and 280A. Section 262 is titled: *Disallowance of Personal, Living, and Family Expenses*. Section 280A is titled: *Disallowance of Certain Expenses* [Re] *Rental of Vacation Homes, Etc.* Both sections carry the identical lead-in clause which reads—

Except as otherwise expressly provided [herein] . . .

The clear inference is that there are some allowable deductions . . . but not many.

Subsection 262(a) reads in full as—

Except as otherwise expressly provided in this chapter [General Rule for Disallowance of Deductions], *no deduction shall be allowed for personal, living, or family expenses.*

This is succinct, emphatic, and clear. The IRS will try to stop you with this rule at every chance it can. Its version of what constitutes personal expenses is extreme and unrealistic. The only "give" by the IRS is on matters of property taxes, mortgage interest, and casualty losses. Other sections of the tax code clearly authorize these three "premier-type" deductions for all forms of property: vacation and nonvacation alike.

Subsection 280A(a) reads in pertinent part—

Except as otherwise provided [herein] . . ., *no deduction otherwise allowable . . . shall be allowed with respect to the use of a dwelling unit which is used by the taxpayer during the taxable year as a residence.*

Subsection 280A(d)(1) defines use "as a residence" as being more than 14 days throughout the year.

Why 14 days? Why not 15, 20, or some other number?

Because 14 days is two weeks. Two weeks is the average length of a paid vacation for most U.S. taxpayers. If one buys a dwelling unit for purely vacation reasons, he certainly wants to enjoy personal use of that property for at least 14 days of the year. Hence, the tax characterization: Vacation home rental rules.

If De Minimis Rental Use

There is a fundamental reason why owners of vacation property rent the use of their property to others. They want some help in defraying its cost and upkeep. The property is customarily vacant most of the year. When it is not being used personally, why not rent it to others to pick up a few dollars?

If the amount of rental use is **less than** 15 days — the approximate equivalent to your own vacation use — a special de minimis rule applies. The term "de minimis," as you know, refers to an amount which is so small as to make accounting for it unreasonable or impracticable. With regard to vacation property, Section 280A(g) addresses this particular point.

Section 280A(g) is titled: *Special Rule for Certain Rental Use.* It reads in full as follows:

8-3

Notwithstanding any other provision of this section or section 183 [relating to not-for-profit activities], *if a dwelling unit is used during the taxable year as a residence* **and** *such dwelling unit is* **actually rented for less than 15 days** *during the taxable year, then—*

> *(1) no deduction otherwise allowable because of the rental use of such dwelling unit shall be allowed, and*
>
> *(2)* **the income derived** *from such use for the taxable year* **shall not be included** *in the gross income of such taxpayer under section 61* [relating to gross income defined]. [Emphasis added.]

The emphasized phrase "actually rented" refers to **fair rental days** only. If you rent your vacation property at competitive market rates for less than 15 days, you *do not* have to include the rental receipts on your Form 1040 tax return. Nor can you claim any expense deductions either.

It is unlikely that you would rent to strangers at below fair market rates. But what happens if you rent to family, friends, and neighbors at below market rates?

The answer is that days rented at below market rates do not count as fair rental days. That is, they are not part of the "less than 15 day" count in Section 280A(g). They count as personal use days. For all personal use days, your only allowable deductions are property taxes and mortgage interest (and casualty losses, if any).

Suppose, now, you rented to friends and family at rates deliberately set below fair market, but sufficient to just offset your expenses other than property taxes and mortgage interest. We include in these expenses such items as insurance, repairs, supplies, cleaning, utilities, association dues, etc. What would be the effect then?

The whole affair would be a *tax wash*. No tax reporting of the rental receipts, nor of the rental expenses, would be required. This could be stretching the de minimis rule a bit, but why not? You are generating no net income for the IRS to tax. You may be satisfied with just this approach. If so, Figure 8.1 may be helpful to you.

Establishing Fair Rental Rate

Once you get a taste of receiving some rental income from your vacation property, you may want to go beyond the tax wash concept in Figure 8.1. You may want to up your rent and rent it

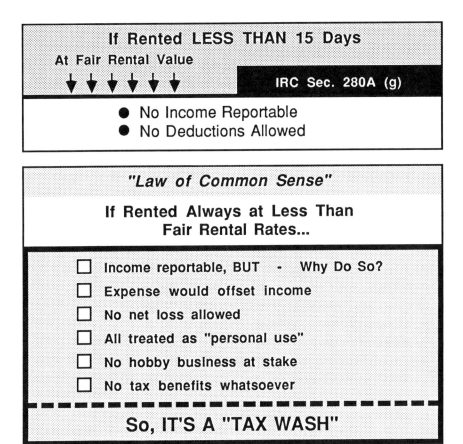

Fig. 8.1 - The "Tax Wash" Concept for Vacation Property Renting

more than 14 days at full fair market rates. When you do this, you are crossing the threshold into the profit motive domain. Now, you have to accurately tax account for all of your rental receipts and rental expenses.

To start the tax accounting, you first have to understand the concept of "fair rental." This is the amount which your vacation property would rent to the general public under competitive market conditions. It presumes that there are other property owners in your vacation area who also may be renting to the public The concept further presumes that the fair rental value in the summertime could well differ from that in the wintertime. There also could be day-today fluctuations, such as during weekdays and on weekends. Hence, the **rental day** aspect.

"How does one determine a fair rental rate?" you ask.

One way is to canvass the general area where your vacation property (dwelling unit or pleasure vehicle) is located, and make direct inquiry to those owners who are also renting out their property to the general public. Or. you can look through the "For Rent" ads in local newspapers and on public bulletin boards.

Probably a better way to document fair rental value is to visit one or more rental agencies in the vicinity of your property. Ask for copies of whatever listings they have on properties currently rented or available for rent. Pay an appraisal fee, and have at least one rental agency prepare a fair rental statement for you. Make sure the statement includes a description of your property, and the number of days out of 365 days per year that you intend to offer it for rent. Have the appraisal statement specify the peak rental months and the low rental months. In popular vacation areas, the peak rental rates may be as much as five times the off-peak (low demand) months. You will need this kind of information to prove to some skeptical IRS agent that you are indeed charging a fair rental rate. You are not "cooking the books" just to show a net rental loss for tax purposes.

Once you establish a fair rental rate for your vacation dwelling unit (cabin, camper, condo) or for your vacation pleasure vehicle (airplane, boat, dune buggy), your next chore is to set up a rental-use log. For dwelling units, you'll rent them by the day or week. For pleasure vehicles, you'll rent them by the hour and, on occasion, for a day or two. For each renter from whom you collect money, list that person's name, address, and amount collected. Otherwise, because vacation properly always carries with it a tax stigma, there could be suspicion that you are allowing family and friends to use it free or at below market rate.

If you want the tax benefits of deducting your legitimate expenses, you are expected to put forth the necessary effort to establish and keep track of your fair rental receipts.

The 14 Day or 10% Rule

For renting any kind of property in a hobby business, the tax form to be used is Schedule E (1040): *Supplemental Income and Loss*. Its Part I accommodates up to three separate rental properties at a time. On line 2 thereof, there is a trigger question which reads—

For each property listed on line 1, did you or your family use it for personal purposes for more than the greater of 14 days or 10% of the total days rented at fair rental value during the tax year? ☐ *Yes* ☐ *No*.

If you answer "Yes," you have officially declared that your property was used substantially for vacation purposes. Therefore, no matter what your allocable rental expenses are, they cannot exceed your rental income. In other words, the bottom line on Schedule E for that property (for which you answered "Yes") must be zero or positive. It cannot be negative. This means that you cannot show a net rental loss.

If you answer "No" to the 14 day-10% question, then your rental expenses, if properly substantiated, can indeed exceed your rental income. This means that you can show a net rental loss on Schedule E for that property.

The trick to being able to answer "No" with a clear conscience is understanding what constitutes personal-use days for the 14 day-10% rule. If you use the property personally for no more than 14 days or no more than 10% of the actual fair rental days, it is tax treated as income-producing property rather than as pure vacation property. Your tax hands are not tied as severely as with a "Yes" answer.

A "day" for vacation rule tax purposes is not necessarily a full 24-hour day. It is *any part* of a day for which the indicated property is used for personal purposes. Using for personal purposes means eating there, sleeping there, or entertaining there for as little as one hour of a day. It excludes eating box lunches and using toilet facilities while there on a bona fide repair and maintenance visit. Sleeping there overnight while on a maintenance visit would constitute personal use. Working there but sleeping elsewhere would not constitute a personal-use day.

The trigger question phrase "you or your family" includes also certain nonfamily persons. A nonfamily person is any person or entity with an ownership interest in the property, or who has an interest in other like-kind property where you or your family can trade vacation stays.

The 10% part of the trigger question is to preempt against your letting family, friends, and others use the alleged rental property free of charge, or at a fee below its fair rental market value. If you do allow this kind of use, each less-than-fair-rental day constitutes a personal-use day.

In Figure 8.2, we try to depict the importance of this 14 day-10% trigger concept. But we caution you, even with a "No" answer, some deduction restrictions apply (as you'll see later).

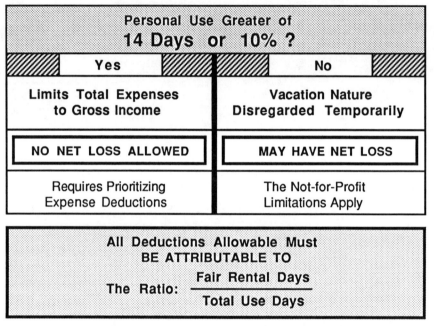

Fig. 8.2 - Different Results When Answering "Yes" or "No"

Expenses Attributable to Rental

Section 280A(e): Expenses Attributable to [Fair] Rental, constitutes the core essence of the vacation property rental rules. The "essence clause" is that the expenses allowable—

Shall not exceed an amount which bears the same relationship to such expenses as the number of days during each year that the unit (or portion thereof) is rented at a fair rental, bears to the total number of days during such year that the unit (or portion thereof) is used.

What is this subsection (e) of 280A really trying to say?

It is trying to say that those "expenses attributable to the rental" must be apportioned by the ratio of the number of fair rental days to the **total use days** for the year. Vacant days in a 365-day year do not count. Subsection (e)(2) does provide an exception to the no-count vacant days for property taxes, mortgage interest, and casualty losses. These items are allowable as personal deductions, irrespective of the above apportionment ratio.

Expressed more straightforwardly, there is an Applicable Expense Ratio (AER) that applies to each expense total for the year. This ratio is:

$$AER = \frac{\text{Number of Fair Rental Days}}{\substack{\text{Total Use Days (fair rental, plus personal use,} \\ \text{plus below-market rentals)}}}$$

To illustrate, suppose that you, your family, and below-market others used the vacation home for 31 days out of the year. Your fair rental diary shows that you actually rented it for 185 days. What is your tax-qualified AER (Applicable Expense Ratio)?

It is—

$$\frac{185}{185+31} = \frac{185}{216} = 0.8564$$
$$\text{or } 85.64\%$$

Thus, you would multiply **all** of your vacation property expenses by this AER. This includes property taxes, mortgage interest, and depreciation. For the example days cited, your unallowed rental expenses would be about 15% of your annual totals.

BUT, in the example cited, you used the vacation property 31 days. This is more than the 14 day-10% rule. Hence, you must answer "Yes" to the trigger question and limit your rental expenses to your rental income. This is Figure 8.2 revisited.

Suppose you reduced your personal-use days from 31 to 16 . . . for the same 185 fair rental days. The number 16 is less than 10% of your fair rental days (10% x 185 days = 18.5 days). In this case, the AER factor would not apply. You would then get 100% of your applicable expenses (AER x actual). You would get these expenses even if they produced a net rental loss. Do you now see the power of the 14 day-10% trigger rule?

Back to "Square One"

Do not get too excited about being able to claim a net loss on your vacation rentals. There is a special throwback trap when you correctly answer "No" to the trigger question. The trap is set in subsection 280A(f)(3): *Coordination With Section 183*. Section 183 — if you will recall our Chapter 2 — is the not-for-profit rule. This is what we mean by "back to square one."

Subsection 280A(f)(3)(B) addresses your no-vacation vacation property rental loss this way:

Such [loss] *year shall be taken into account as a taxable year for purposes of applying subsection (d) of Section 183 (relating to the 5-year presumption).*

In other words, a legitimate net loss from the renting of vacation property may be tax recognized only for two years out of a 5-consecutive-year period. After these two loss years, you have to prove (pursuant to our Chapter 4) that you have full intentions of making a profit. You may be able to show this intention quite readily, if you plan to sell the property within the next few years . . . when the market is ripe. Vacation dwelling units (not so for pleasure vehicles) often appreciate in value, as the population of the world increases.

The IRS's rationale for its throwback stance is that you rented a vacation home; there was no profit motive when you bought it. Therefore, the not-for-profit rules (of Section 183) apply. The only concession you get is that your unallowable attributable losses can be carried over to a subsequent fair rental tax year. The supposition is that you may want to increase your rents the following year.

Which unallowed attributable losses are carried over? There's a 3-step priority procedure to follow. We portray this priority sequence in Figure 8.3.

Priority 1 uses property taxes and mortgage interest to reduce your rental income (designated as *Class I* expenses). Priority 2 uses your operating expenses (insurance, repairs, utilities, etc.) to reduce your rental income (designated as *Class II* expenses). And Priority 3 is your scheduled depreciation (designated as *Class III* expenses). At whatever point in this reduction hierarchy your net income reduces to zero, your remaining unusable deductions are disallowed . . . for that year. You then have the task of keeping track of your

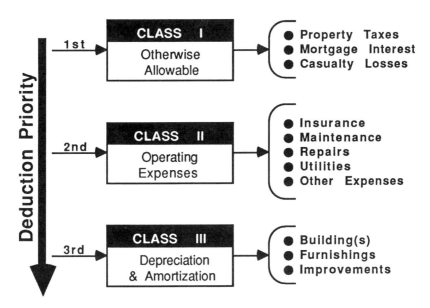

Fig. 8.3 - Expense Classifications for Prioritizing Deductions

attributable unallowed losses for possibly using them in subsequent years.

Qualified Rental Periods

If all of the above is too much for you, and you are serious about wanting to rent your vacation property for profit, there is a practical way out. List your property with an established rental agency. Sign a rental contract for no less than 12 consecutive months. Have the rental agency do all the advertising, collect all rents, pay all operating expenses, and report to you periodically the net cash proceeds, if any. Your rental contract should specify that any cash shortage is made up by you (which is tax deductible). Taxwise, this arrangement is treated as a *qualified rental period*.

Let us explain.

If you rent your vacation home under conditions called a "qualified rental period," you need not establish fair rental days. Nor do personal-use days become a tax-qualifying concern. You may use the property all you want before or after the qualified rental period . . . but not during it.

As per subsection 280A(d)(4)(B), the term qualifying rental period means—

A consecutive period of—
(i) 12 or more months which begins or ends in [the] *taxable year, or*
*(ii) less than 12 months which begins in such taxable year and at the end of which such dwelling unit is sold or exchanged, and—for which such unit is rented **or is held for rental**, at a fair rental.* [Emphasis added.]

A consecutive 12-month period "held for rental" would be your entering into an enforceable rental-listing contract with an established rental firm. By so doing, the tax law rationale is that you have knowingly converted your vacation home into bona fide rental property seeking a profit. Thereupon, the vacation property (attributable expense) rental rules would not apply.

As with any rental-listing contract, there will be bona fide periods of nonrental. There will be off-season vacancies, and short-term vacancies between old tenants moving out and new tenants moving in. During these nonrental periods, should you visit the property to do cleaning, painting, repairs, and maintenance, such visits would not count as personal use.

Strategy for Selling

Many taxpayers buy vacation property more or less in synchronism with the physical development and social activity stages of their children. They may buy (and hold) a dwelling unit and/or pleasure vehicle in one vacation area for a few years, then sell and buy in another vacation area later. As a family, the vacation needs of children (as well as of the parents) will differ for young children, teenagers, and young adults. As the children mature and get married, and grandchildren come along, the grandparents seek a different vacation area with different facilities. The point we are making is that vacation property, particularly a dwelling unit, is seldom held for more than five to 10 years at a time. Even at time of purchase it is known that it will be sold one day.

There is a definite tax strategy for selling vacation property. It is a two-pronged strategy depending on whether the property is real estate or nonrealty property. Schedule E real estate is that which is fixed to land; nonrealty is mobile or vehicular in type. Thus, such property as cabins, condos, and cottages would be realty, whereas motor homes, campers, yachts, airplanes, and dune buggies would be nonrealty. As is often the case, realty (property fixed to land) tends to appreciate in market value over time. In contrast, vehicular property (nonrealty) almost always depreciates in value over time. As a result, entirely two different strategies arise when selling your vacation property.

We depict these two planning strategies in Figure 8.4, and explain them below. When selling appreciated property (fixed to land), list it with a qualified broker in the area of its location. If you

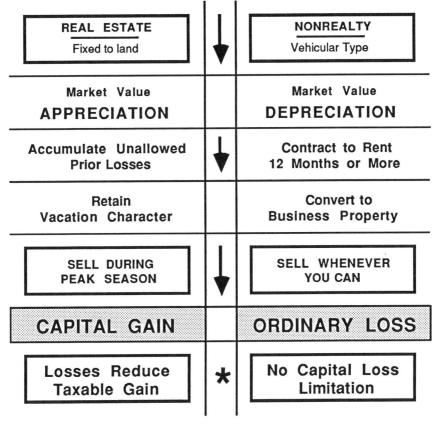

Fig. 8.4 - Preplanning Strategies for Selling Vacation Property

list it off-season, authorize the broker to rent it (if he can) so as to help defray some of your expenses until sold. If the sale results in a capital gain, all of your "attributable unallowed (rental) losses" of the past can be used to offset some of the gains on the sale proceeds. The net result is that you pay less tax on your actual capital gain.

Before selling vacation property which has depreciated in market value (vehicular type, mostly), list it for rent with a reputable agency. At the very minimum, you want it offered to the public for rent for 12 consecutive months. Better yet, have the rental period span one full tax year. This means that you would start the rental contract prior to January 1 and would terminate after December 31. This would give you a "full rental year" for tax reporting purposes.

The reason for a full rental year is to show that you have intentionally converted your former vacation property to rental income property. As such, it becomes tax classed as "business" property. The vacation property loss limitation rules no longer apply. When you sell business property at a loss, it is tax treated as an *ordinary loss*: NOT a capital loss. An ordinary loss is not statutorily limited in amount as is the case with a capital loss. If there are no other capital gains for the year, a capital loss is limited to $3,000 per year.

All vacation property, be it fixed or vehicular, should be acquired with its selling strategies in mind. If for no other reason, preplanned selling gives you a leg up on the profit motive criteria.

9

RESEARCH & EXPLORATION

Under Proper Conditions, Your Hobby Business Expenditures For Technological Research And Mineral Exploration Can Be Expensed Rather Than Capitalized. This Is The Gist Of Sec. 174(a) For RESEARCH And Sec. 617(a) For EXPLORATION. The Requisite Conditions Are: (1) Some "Connection" With An Existing Trade Or Business; (2) Active Control Over The R&E Effort; And (3) "Infrastructure" To Exploit The Results Commercially. Deductible Also Is A Depreciation Allowance (Sec. 167) For Machinery And Equipment Used, And A Depletion Allowance (Sec. 613) For Ores And Minerals Extracted From Earth. Individual Entrepreneurs Do Best In High Quality, Low Quantity R&E Efforts.

Prior to 1987, tax shelters were a flourishing business. They flourished because they took advantage of the many sections of the tax code which encouraged research (for new technology products) and exploration (for valued natural resources). These were — still are — high risk ventures requiring substantial upfront money from diverse interests. In many cases, the tax benefits far exceeded the amount of money invested by each participant. Most participants were limited partners, which meant that they were essentially passive investors.

Those tax shelter days are gone. Tax shelters were "put out of business" by the Tax Reform Act of 1986. This was done by imposing new passive loss limitation rules which were "phased in" through 1990. As the result of these new rules, the form of entrepreneurial engagement in research and exploration has changed. The old tax rules have been tightened without destroying the basic incentives of research and exploration.

In this chapter, we want to present a reality approach to hobby ventures in research and exploration. In this regard, we particularly want to address Section 174: Research and Experimental Expenditures, and Sections 617/616: Exploration and Development Expenditures. For the right qualifying taxpayers, these sections permit deducting the expenditures currently rather than capitalizing and amortizing them over time.

As you will see below, Section 174 focuses on *inventors*: those persons who create new technology products for the marketplace. Sections 617/616 focus on *prospectors*: those persons searching for and extracting from our natural resources those materials which are useful in trade or commerce.

Proximate Nexus Required

In the prior chapter ventures, the hobby business could be — and often was — quite unrelated to the livelihood business of the entrepreneur. This is **not** the case with research and exploration activities. There has to be some "close relationship" (proximate nexus) between one's existing livelihood business and his hobby venture. The practical effect is that the hobby venture becomes an extension, or offshoot, or expansion potential of one's existing trade or business.

One reason for this proximate nexus requirement is the profit motive factor. Inventing and prospecting take on the characteristics of a recreational and spare time hobby. Venturers in these fields have a natural curiosity about ways to improve and better their lives. Even when unsuccessful, certain inner satisfaction and personal fulfillment are achieved. Such results in and of themselves are not indicative of the profit motive. But, if undertaken *in connection with* an existing trade or business, where profits (to one degree or another) have been generated year after year, the profit motive "shifts over" to the hobby undertaking.

The more practical reason for the proximate nexus requirement is the extent of the expertise required in research and exploration. A total novice is simply going to waste his time and money in learning the technicalities of the trade.

In the research and experimentation domain, for example, it is highly unlikely that an attorney or accountant would have the technical expertise to invent and develop an acoustic garage door opener. Such a device is activated by the garage owner's auto horn, which is acoustically calibrated to the door opener's sensor. To engage in such an experimental undertaking, one would have to be some combination of an acoustical, electrical, and mechanical engineer He also would have to be in some engineering consulting business, some specialty manufacturing business, or some building installation business. From the experiences in one of these businesses, the need for such a device would most likely emerge on its own.

Similarly, in the exploration and development domain. An insurance salesman or computer programmer would be hard pressed to show a relationship between his livelihood business and the expertise required for prospecting and mining precious stones, for example. One would have to have some profit-making know-how in gemology, crystallography, extractive processes, and the cutting and polishing of rare stones. A more likely venturer would be a custom jeweler with training in mineralogy, geochemistry and, possibly, some precious stone mining experience.

The "Realistic Possibility" Standard

Over the years, the IRS has defeated many taxpayers claiming deductions for their Section 174 (research) and Sections 617/616 (exploration) expenditures. The IRS and the Tax Court have done this by formulating a so-called "realistic possibility" standard. The idea is that when one engages in inventing and prospecting, there must be some realistic likelihood that the end results, if successful, could be used in the trade or business of the venturer (or be licensed to others).

This concept stops just short of requiring that the end results be successful. How can anyone guarantee that some unknown, new, and untried product will be successful in the profit-making sense? The answer, of course, is that one cannot make such a guarantee. Therefore, the realistic possibility standard is predicated upon the premise of: IF the hobby venture is successful.

If the venture is successful, you are expected to be in a position with the wherewithal to commence marketing activities. If you show no inclination or infrastructure to launch your invented device or extracted resource into the market place, all of your Sections 174 and 617/616 expenditures could well be tax denied. This is what happened in the case of *J.R. Harris*, 58 TCM 1441, TC Memo 1990-80.

Harris was a limited partner in a venture to research and develop cementitious compounds (blends of Portland cement with alumina, iron oxide, etc.) for the construction industry. The partnership agreement did not provide that the technology being developed would be exploited in the trade or business of the partnership. The fact that research results were promising was negated by the fact that there were no funds available in the partnership to commence marketing. Consequently, the court ruled that "there was no realistic prospect that the technology would ever be used."

A similar ruling was rendered in the cases of *K.E. Kantor*, 60 TCM 225, TC Memo 1990-380 **and** *J.P. Coleman*, 60 TCM 123, TC Memo 1990-357. In both cases, general partnerships were formed for the research and development activities. In *Kantor*, the effort was directed towards new computer software, whereas in *Coleman* it was towards a better silver recovery process. In both cases, the partnerships did not have the capital nor intent to exploit their works by licensing them to others. An exclusive option by the partners to retain the results unto themselves circumvented any realistic prospect of the results being marketed to others.

Role of Intermediaries

As stated earlier, research and exploration (R&E) activities require significant capital and expertise. The effort also has to be associated with an existing trade or business, out of which there is some likelihood that the results, if successful, will be marketed.

Successful R&E venturers have found that intermediate entities — *general* partnerships, in particular — provide the best transition from old business to new. Each member of the partnership contributes capital, facilities, and talent to the stand-alone entity. The expenditures incurred in the R&E effort are allocated back to the individual partners (in separate businesses of their own) in proportion to each partner's fractional interest in the combined venture. If the venture is successful, the partnership agreement calls for a licensing or some marketing arrangement for exploiting the device or resource developed. This is how many new businesses get started. When ideas are transformed into reality, and the reality is structured in a way to make it an ongoing appendage to our national economy, deductibility of R&E expenditures is pretty much assured.

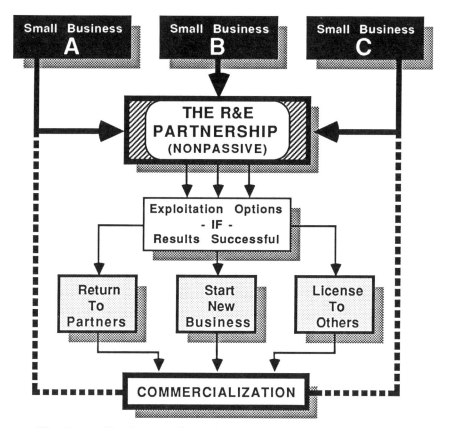

Fig. 9.1 - The Intermediary Role of a Partnership for R&E

The intermediary role of partnerships in R&E ventures is depicted in Figure 9.1. We want to emphasize that the intermediate entity is a general (nonpassive) partnership. No limited partners or limited entrepreneurs are involved. Each member (and his subordinates, if any) participates in the R&E effort in an ongoing and focused way. The clear objective of the entity is to commercialize the results where practical.

Section 174 Overview

Section 174 is officially titled: *Research and Experimental Expenditures*. Its subsection (a) is subtitled: TREATMENT AS EXPENSES. This subsection reads in full as follows:

A taxpayer may treat research or experimental expenditures which are paid or incurred by him during the taxable year in connection with his trade or business as expenses which are not chargeable to capital account. The expenditures so treated **shall be allowed** *as a deduction.* [Emphasis added.]

Section 174(a) is unchanged since its first adoption into law in 1957. That's more than 35 years ago. Yet, today, the IRS still tries to defeat this law by asserting that it doesn't mean what it says. It takes the position that the clause "shall be allowed" (as a currently deductible expense) doesn't really apply because the phrase "research or experimental expenditures" is a judgment call which only the IRS can make. There is also a reasonableness standard which the IRS forced Congress to enact into law in 1989.

Subsection 174(e) empowers the IRS in a dangerous way. It enables the IRS — an agency which is noncreative, nonvisionary, and nonimaginative — to substitute its own judgment for that of an inventor as to what constitutes reasonable expenditures for research and experimentation effort. It reads—

This section [174] *shall apply to a research or experimental expenditure* **only to the extent** *that the amount thereof is reasonable under the circumstances.* [Emphasis added.]

The Congressional Committee Report [P.L. 101-239] which sponsored subsection 174(e) states—

The committee does not intend that the reasonableness requirement under section 174 be used to question whether or not research activities themselves are of a reasonable type or nature. . . . [only] *that the amounts supposedly paid for research . . .* [not be] *disguised as dividends, gifts, loans, or other similar payments.*

Even this statement of Congressional intent invites the IRS to ask a lot of questions in its drive to defeat the expense mandate of Section 174(a). It tries to dissuade a taxpayer from using 174(a) by forcing him to use subsection (b) [amortization over 60 months] or subsection (f) [amortization over 10 years (120 months)]. If a taxpayer does not succumb to its intimidation pressures, the IRS then disallows the expenditure deductions altogether. This forces the taxpayer into Tax Court to implement his interpretation of Section 174(a).

Regulation 1.174-2: Definitions

Regulation 1.174-2(a)(1) defines the term "research or experimental expenditures" as—

[Those] *expenditures incurred in connection with the taxpayer's trade or business which represent research and development costs in the experimental or laboratory sense. The term includes generally all such costs incident to the development of an experimental or pilot model, a plant process, a product, a formula, an invention, or similar property, and the improvement of already existing property of the type mentioned. The term does not include expenditures such as those for the ordinary testing or inspection of materials or products for quality control or those for efficiency surveys, management studies, consumer surveys, advertising, or promotions. However, the term includes the costs of obtaining a patent, such as attorneys' fees in making and perfecting a patent application. On the other hand, the term does not include the costs of acquiring another's patent, model, production or process, nor does it include expenditures paid or incurred for research in connection with literary, historical, or similar projects.*

Whew!

Now you know how the IRS can interpret "research or experimental expenditures" any way it wants. In those product and service areas where new ideas are untried or unproven, there's a judgment call to be made. Whenever there is a judgment call, the IRS will always rule against the taxpayer, except in the case of a large corporation. Large corporations have their own separate research and development divisions where the type of R&D programs have been pretty well thrashed out by intervening management committees.

Regulation 1.174-2(b)(1) goes on to say that—

Expenditures by the taxpayer for the acquisition or improvement of land, or for the acquisition or improvement of property which is subject to an allowance for depreciation under section 167 or depletion under section 611, are not deductible under section

174, irrespective of the fact that the property or improvements may be used by the taxpayer in connection with research and experimentation.

What these regulatione are saying is that the results of the R&D effort must be made available for commercialization to others. Land and its improvements, and equipment and machinery retained in the business, are not the types of commercialization envisioned.

Hardware vs. Software

The core issue over the deductibility of Section 174(a) expenditures boils down to whether the end product of the research and experimentation is hardware or software. If it is an item of hardware capable of being marketed, there seems to be little controversy that its R&D expenses are deductible. The size and price of the marketed item is irrelevant. It could be a hand-held saline water conversion kit, or a huge supersonic prototype aircraft. If it is hardware and marketable, it comes within the expense option of Section 174(a) and does not have to be capitalized.

In contrast, if the end product of the R&D is software, a whole different interpretation ballgame arises. This is because there are many kinds of software, some associated with hardware and some not. Patentable-type software such as a patent itself, process formula, or plant design are generally accepted as Section 174(a) expenditures. Copyrightable software such as a copyright itself, technical textbook, or technology encyclopedia are always disallowed under Section 174(a). The rationale seems to be that these items are literary compositions and historical treatises which are of a lower level of creativity than patentable items.

What about computer software? Some is patentable; some is copyrightable. What is the Section 174(a) distinction here?

The IRS has addressed the R&D expenditures issue of computer software programs. It issued Revenue Procedure 69.21 (1969-2, CB 303) in which it said—

"Computer software" includes all programs or routines used to cause a computer to perform a desired task or set of tasks, and the documents required to describe and maintain those programs. Computer programs of all classes, for example, operating systems, executive systems, monitors, compilers and translators, assembly routines, and utility programs as well as

*application programs are included. "Computer software" does **not include procedures which are external to computer operations**, such as instructions to transcription operators and external control procedures.* [Emphasis added.]

The costs of developing software (whether or not the particular software is patented or copyrighted) in many respects so closely resemble the kind of research and experimental expenditures that fall within the purview of Section 174 . . . as to warrant accounting treatment similar to that accorded such costs under that section.

In other words, the costs of developing software that relates to the **internal workings** of computer hardware — or to any other kind of hardware — is fully deductible under Section 174(a). If the software relates to the **external** use of computers — or to any other information source, it is not deductible. To summarize our perception of this Section 174(a) treatment, we present Figure 9.2.

Overview of Sections 617/616

Section 617 of the tax code addresses exploration expenditures in connection with natural resources, whereas Section 616 addresses development expenditures of those resources which have been found. You can't develop a resource until you've first found it. Therefore, logic would suggest that Section 616 should address exploration matters and that Section 617 should address development matters. Or, better yet, the two should be incorporated in one section (exploration *and* development), similar to Section 174 (research *and* experimentation). But logic is not what tax law is all about: "convoluted thinking" is.

Section 617 is officially titled: ***Deduction and Recapture of Certain Mining Exploration Expenditures.*** Immediately, you should sense something unusual here: "deduction and *recapture*"? The general rule, subsection (a), reads as follows:

*At the election of the taxpayer, expenditures paid or incurred during the taxable year for the purpose of ascertaining the **existence, location, extent, or quality** of any deposit of ore or other mineral, and paid or incurred **before the** beginning of the **development stage** of the mine, shall be allowed as a deduction in computing taxable income.* [Emphasis added.]

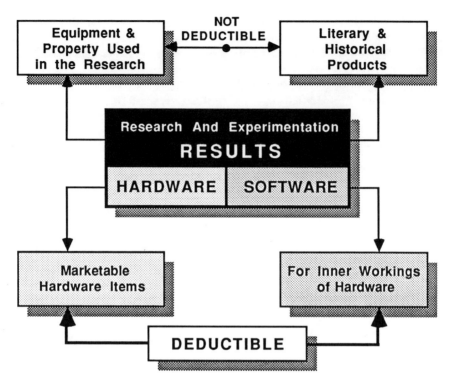

Fig. 9.2 - The Deductibility of Sec. 174 (a) Expenditures

Compare this wording with that in the general rule, subsection (a) of Section 616: *Development Expenditures.* Its first sentence reads—

*Except as provided in subsections (b) and (d), there shall be allowed as a deduction in computing taxable income all expenditures paid or incurred during the taxable year for the development of a mine or other natural deposit (other than an oil or gas well) if paid or incurred **after the existence** of ores or minerals in **commercially marketable quantities** has been disclosed.* [Emphasis added.]

The phrases "at the election of" in Section 617(a) and "except as provided" in Section 616(a) represent our concept of convoluted thinking. Section 617(a) refers you to its subsection (b) where you have to **recapture** the expensed amounts when you reach the production stage. This means that you include in production income that which you expensed during the exploratory years. Section 616(a) also refers you to its subsection (b) where you have to **defer and amortize** your expensed amounts when you reach the production stage. This means that you recapture your development expenditures ratably over the units of production sold over the mine's commercial lifetime. There is something noticeably silent in this convoluted thinking process. What happens to your expensed expenditures for exploration and development if you never reach the mine production stage?

This is where the Section 183 profit motive comes in, and where some connection to an existing trade or business is essential. To the IRS's way of thinking, Sections 617/616 mandate that you reach the production stage, and produce commercially marketable quantities, otherwise your previously expensed deductions are summarily disallowed. If you are lucky, you may be allowed to amortize the expenditures over five years or so.

Small Business Prospects

Sections 617/616 both have provisions which exclude oil, gas, and geothermal exploration and development (E&D) expenses. This exclusion results from the fact that another more applicable provision of the tax code applies, namely: Section 263(c). This section is titled: *Intangible Drilling and Development Costs in the Case of Oil and Gas Wells and Geothermal Wells.* Oil, gas, and geothermal energy exploitation is necessarily — because of stringent environmental impact studies — a very large-scale operation. It is our contention, therefore, that oil and gas E&D is an unlikely area for entrepreneurial activity by hobby business venturers.

More likely, small businesses would find their rewards in small-scale operations involving—

1. precious metals (for dental and plating activities)
2. precious gems (for jewelry and gift shop activities)
3. precious sands (for glass and tableware activities)
4. precious clays (for roof tile and pottery activities)
5. precious stones (for fireplaces and decorative construction)

. . . and other similar high quality (hence, the term "precious"), low quantity, natural resources.

In our citations of Sections 617(a)/616(a) above, we have only "touched the surface" of the tax ramifications that await the small business prospector. For example, before engaging in any kind of E&D operation, certain intangible (nonphysical) expenditures are required. There are costs for rights of way, access permits, lease rights, surface rights, subsurface rights, mineral rights, topographical surveys, impact studies, and other compliances with Federal, state, and local regulations regarding natural deposits. These costs are treated as preparatory capital costs; they are NOT E&D-type expenditures which Sections 617(a)/616(a) envision. These preparatory costs have to be capitalized and recovered when the property interest is sold.

E&D costs, which can be expensed currently, are those which are limited strictly to the **physical activities** of finding a mineral and developing it. Several recent Tax Court cases have clarified the general concepts here.

For example, in *J.A. Levert* [57 TCM 910], the court held that—

> *Payments made to a contractor for aerial and surface reconnaissance, surface and underground mapping, sampling, and the collection of data were deductible as exploration expenditures.*

In *P.R. Schouten* [61 TCM 2357], the court denied a deduction for development expenses because—

> *The taxpayer failed to prove that there were any minerals located in the mine in question. 'Mine development expenses' refers to activity necessary to make a deposit accessible for mining.*

And in *M.E. Anderson* [83 TC 898], the court held that—

> *The taxpayers could not deduct amounts paid to a consulting geologist, allegedly for mining development expenses, because there was no development of the mine to which the taxpayers had staked their claim.*

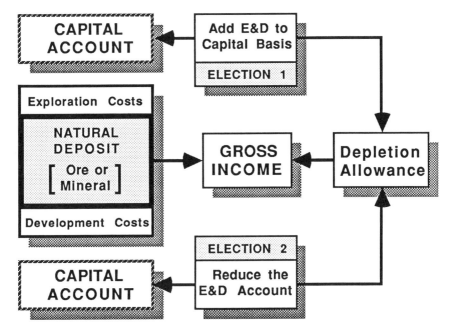

Fig. 9.3 - The Recapture Elections of Mining E&D

Depletion Allowance & Recapture

Depletion is a tax allowance for the extraction and exhaustion of natural ores and minerals from earth. The allowance is a prescribed percentage of the gross income of the mining operation each year. The percentage rate is set forth in Section 613(b): *Percentage Depletion Rates*. The rate varies from a low of 5% (for common gravel, stone, and clay) to a high of 22% (for quartz, graphite, and heavy metals).

Once a developed mine reaches the production stage, including all treatment processes, the role of depletion allowance comes into play. At this point, we revert back to "square one": the **recapture** of E&D. That is, all cumulative prior E&D costs which have been expensed are "added back" to the capital (investment) basis in the mine. A taxpayer has to show on his return one of two recapture elections (which we depict in Figure 9.3).

Recapture Election 1 is where a taxpayer totals all of his previous E&D costs (which he expensed), and simply adds them to the amount of unrecovered capital he has invested in the mine. Once he does this, he is then free to claim the prescribed percentage depletion allowance against all productive income from the mine. However, he has to separately track his cumulative depletion allowances for offset accounting purposes.

Recapture Election 2 is where a taxpayer totals his prior E&D costs as in Election 1. Instead of adding these costs directly to his capital basis, he sets up a separate recapture account on the side. He reduces this account by the amount of the depletion allowance which he otherwise would be entitled to, year after year. He does **not** deduct this allowance from his gross income each year, as in the case of Election 1.

There is a tax theory behind E&D recapture of costs with respect to natural resources. The theory is that all E&D expenditures are really part of the "manufacturing cost" of producing a physical item for sale. When an item is produced and marketed, and income is derived, only then is a ratable portion of the E&D costs recovered. This recoverability is the role of the depletion allowance.

When a mining interest is disposed of (by sale, abandonment, destruction, seizure, or other termination of income rights) the nonrecovered E&D costs either reduce the capital gain or increase the ordinary loss from the hobby business venture. There also could be a pure abandonment loss. This is where Form 4797 (Sales of Business Property) comes into use. We introduced Form 4797 to you back in Chapter 5 (commencing on page 5-7).

10

SPORTS, TRAVEL, & THEATRICS

> Using Section 274: DISALLOWANCE, Etc., The IRS Too Often Makes Snap Judgments Against Hobby Businesses Involving Entertainment, Amusement, Or Recreation. Until You Can Demonstrate Profit Motive, You Need To Foil IRS's Fetish With Nonimplicative Business Names, Activity Codes, And Sales Literature. Study The Schedule C Instructions And Check-boxes Carefully For Those Years In Which You Show NET LOSS. Three Or More Consecutive Loss Years Will Computer-Trigger Your Return(s) For Audit. Although Various Court Decisions Reveal That The IRS Can Be Wrong, It Nevertheless Continues Its Mindset Against Sports, Travel, And Theatrics.

Unlike inventing and prospecting (research and exploration), there are no special tax rules that provide incentives for hobby businesses involving sports, travel, and theatrics. Quite the contrary. There is one particular rule that is purposely designed to discourage engagement in said activities. This rule is Section 274: Disallowance of Certain Entertainment, Etc. Expenses. We'll tell you more about Section 174 later. In the meantime, we have a few definitional terms to explain.

When we use the term "sports," we are referring to those nonprofessional sporting-type events where you may participate directly or indirectly . . . mostly indirectly. As a hobby business venturer, you offer a product or service that relates in some way to a particular sport. Your direct participation, if any, is just enough to give you the "hands on" experience to better the product or service that you introduce. In other words, you are not a professional sportsman, nor is your engagement in the sporting activity for your own recreation. There is a genuine business motive to your endeavors.

Similarly, when we use the term "travel," we are referring to a type of business in which you offer a product or service to those who do travel. While you yourself may travel occasionally, the purpose is to improve your expertise and knowledge. It is not an opportunity for a tax deductible vacation for you and your family.

Also, similarly, when we use the term "theatrics," we are referring to a type of business in which nonprofessionals — amateurs, if you will — perform as entertainers. This is the realm of the "performing arts" in entertainment, amusement, and recreation. While you may be a part-time performer yourself, your hobby business is primarily aimed at those who do perform (more or less regularly).

The idea of a hobby business being related to sports, travel, and theatrics smacks up against an age-old tax taboo. That taboo is: *Thou shalt not derive any pleasure, amusement, or recreation* from those activities in which you seek tax deduction benefits. Accordingly, in this chapter we hope to present some constructive suggestions for circumventing the ruthless tax bias that so often prevails.

Foiling the Hawk Eye

Imagine yourself as a high-flying hawk, eagle, or falcon soaring over masses of hobby business taxpayers. From a little computer chip in your memory brain, a rhythmic message keeps beeping forth: "disallow," "disallow," "disallow." The message is harmonically interposed with the subliminal words: *pleasure*; *amusement*; *recreation*: disallow, disallow, disallow.

As you soar over those Form 1040 filers of hobby businesses, the optical wavelengths in your hawk eye suddenly lock on to your prey. You swoop down, snatch your prey, and automatically disallow all tax deductions. That little computer chip then sends out a "snip, snip" signal . . . and you feel good. You have denied all deductions for any business that is "contaminated" with your visions of pleasure, amusement, or recreation.

This is **exactly the way** the IRS approaches any hobby business containing the elements of sports, travel, and theatrics. It has an uncanny eagle eye for spotting these features in your business name, business practice, and business activity code.

Fortunately, there is a foiling technique that you can use against the IRS. It requires, however, that there be bona fide substance to your business activity. The technique is to choose a business name that implies hard work, disciplined study, deep thinking, and physical agony. The name you choose, in and of itself, must not suggest in any way that there is one iota of pleasure, amusement, recreation, or entertainment in your activity. The purpose of your business must be to produce revenue for government: not recreation for yourself.

Suppose, for example, that you are a meteorologist with an international airline. One of your fringe benefits is free airline passes worldwide. During your off-duty times (weekends, vacations, sick leaves) you hike and explore fossil forests worldwide. You search, poke, and dig for a particular kind of amber (hardened tree resin) that has entombed insects and plants. Over the years of doing this as a pure hobby, you have acquired a high degree of expertise and knowledge. You have developed methods for making maps of old forests where fossilized amber can be found. You have also developed your own tools and instruments for sorting and assaying the finds that you make. From your various contacts, you learn that amateur paleontology (study of fossils) is a fast-growing avocation for outdoor-type travelers and hikers worldwide. You discover a market niche and start your own business. What do you name it?

You could call it—

"Amber World & Trees" (or)
"Amber Maps International" (or)
"Travel Pointers to Fossil Forests"

But don't these names sound more like fun than hard work? "World"; "International"; "Travel" — surely there is pleasure and recreation implied. Old hawk-eye — the IRS — will pounce on you.

But, suppose you named your hobby business—

"Amber Maps & Tools"

Would not the term "amber" imply some mystic value for making money? Would not the term "map" imply a folded sheet of paper that has to be read and studied? And, would not the term "tools" imply manual dexterity and hard work?

This is what we mean by foiling the hawk eye. You are not trying to mislead. You are just trying to get past the initial mindset of the IRS when making snap judgments as to your hobby business motives.

Schedule C Headlines

Schedule C (1040) is **the** tax form to use when reporting income and expenses in connection with hobby businesses of the type addressed in this chapter (as well as in the next). As indicated back in Chapter 5 (Figure 5.3) its title is: *Profit OR Loss From Business* (Sole Proprietorship). A small print headnote which follows this title says—

See Instructions for Schedule C (Form 1040).

The foiling technique we illustrated above actually derives from these official instructions.

There are four entry headlines on Schedule C which set the stage for allowability — or disallowability — of your expense entries later. We present these headlines in Figure 10.1. First to note is the space labeled: "Name of proprietor." It does **not** say: "proprietors" (plural). Thus, even though you may file a Form 1040 joint return, Schedule C is a *per person* form. This is emphasized by the fact that there is only sufficient space for entering **one** social security number: that of the sole proprietor alone.

The particular headline spaces in Figure 10.1 that we want to address are: A, B, and C. These spaces are labeled:

A — Principal business
B — Activity code
C — Business name

As to headlining your principal business (space A), the instructions read in pertinent part—

Describe the business or professional activity that provided your principal source of income reported on . . . [Gross receipts or sales]. Give the general field or activity and the type of product or service. . . . also give the type of customer or client.

Schedule C (Form 1040)	Profit OR Loss From Business	
Name of proprietor		Soc. Sec. No.
A. Principal Business		B. Activity Code
C. Business Name		Employer I.D.
Business Address		

Fig. 10.1 - The Vital Headlines on Schedule C

Using this instruction, you could describe your amber maps and tools business above as—

"Sales & Service: Hardware & Software to Paleontologists."

The "hardware" could be those tools and instruments that you had someone else manufacture to your specifications. The "software" could be your maps, guidebooks, and instructions for amber cutting and polishing. But this is probably overdoing things. Besides, how many IRS personnel would know what a "paleontologist" does? It is much simpler to say—

Sales & Service: Amber Maps & Tools

When you use the term "sales & service" without giving any customer description, your customer base is construed as being the general public. This connotation diverts attention from the adverse tax implications of pleasure, amusement, or recreation.

Selection of "Business Code"

On the reverse side of Schedule C (which is page 2), the IRS lists some 185 different 4-digit code numbers characterizing your principal business activity. The list is headed: *Principal Business or Professional Activity Codes*. The instructions at the head of the list say—

Locate the major category that best describes your activity. Within the major category, select the activity code that most closely identifies the business or profession that is the principal source of your sales or receipts. **Enter this 4-digit code on page 1, line B.**

The IRS has identified 25 major categories of businesses. The category most suitable to this chapter is—

Amusement & Recreational Services

Within this category, there are such 4-digit businesses as:

Bowling centers	**9670**
Physical fitness facilities	**8557**
Sports & racing	**9696**
Theatrical performers	**9811**
Musicians & others	**9837**

A hobby venturer who voluntarily classifies himself into one of the "Amusement & Recreational" codes takes on a big risk. He is bound to trigger off the IRS's computer chips chirping: "disallow," "disallow," "disallow." For livelihood businesses, the 4-digit code-triggered disallowance routine is not nearly so great

It is significant to note, for example, that of the 185 codified business classes, not one uses the word "travel." Nor do we find the word "amber," or "maps," or "tools." How would you 4-digitize these or other IRS-uncodified hobby businesses?

Answer: If you look beyond the Amusement & Recreational category, you'll find two catchall possibilities. These are:

Code 7880 — Other business services
Code 8888 — Unable to classify

Why not use one of these 4-digit codes when truly in doubt?

The instructions tell you to enter your selected 4-digit code in the space B indicated on the face of the form (as in Figure 10.1). In contrast, the instructions are totally silent on how you select and enter your business name (space C). Where to enter is obvious. The wording you enter is entirely up to you. So, choose your business name carefully and wisely. Avoid those words which signify amusement, entertainment, or recreation.

Why the Tax Taboo?

Why does the IRS have such an aversion to sports-related, travel-related, and entertainment-related hobby business activities?

Answer: Because the very opening sentence of Section 274 of the Internal Revenue Code says—

No deduction otherwise allowable . . . shall be allowed . . . with respect to . . . entertainment, amusement, or recreation.

The answer is also because the IRS, by its mindset nature, will always disallow under any pretext. Any bureaucracy with the power to say "No" will exercise that power against you, over and over again.

Section 274 is officially titled: ***Disallowance of Certain Entertainment, Etc., Expenses***. It subsection (a) is titled: *Entertainment, Amusement, or Recreation*. Other subsections target gifts, travel (foreign, domestic, and cruise ships), conventions, entertainment tickets, sky boxes (at sports, circus, and theatrical affairs) . . . and so on.

Section 274 — the basic No-No law itself — consists of approximately 8,500 words! The regulations "thereunder" consist of another 15,000 words. This is an example of how the IRS has gone mad. Sure, Congress enacted Section 274, but the IRS was its principal sponsor.

Subsection 274(a)(1)(A), (B) exemplifies what we mean. It reads in part—

No deduction . . . shall be allowed for any item—
(A) With respect to an activity which is of a type generally considered to constitute entertainment, amusement, or recreation, unless the taxpayer establishes that the item was directly related to, or, in the case of an item directly preceding or following a substantial and bona fide business discussion (including business meetings at a convention or otherwise), that such item was associated with, the active conduct of the taxpayer's trade or business, or
(B) With respect to a facility used in connection with an activity referred to in subparagraph (A).

Can you read between the lines? If so, you can see that the principal target of Section 274 is those persons who claim as business expenses their expenditures for sports-related, travel-related, and entertainment-related events. Hobby businesses in these areas, in and of themselves, are not the specific disallowance targets. BUT, the IRS does not make this distinction. It shoots from the hip — without objectivity — at every opportunity it can.

Shooting from the hip by the IRS is further encouraged by such regulations as—

Reg. 1.274-1:   Disallowance of certain entertainment, gift, and travel expenses.

Reg. 1.274-2:   Disallowance of deductions for certain expenses for entertainment, amusement, or recreation.

Reg. 1.274-3:   Disallowance of deductions for gifts.

Reg. 1.274-4:   Disallowance of certain foreign travel expenses.

Just reading the headings of these regulations alone explains why the IRS's computer brain keeps chirping: "disallow," "disallow," "disallow."

Leveling With Customers

Although sports, travel, and entertainment-related hobby businesses are not the direct targets of Section 274, said businesses are indirectly affected. This indirection occurs through one's customers and clients. If a customer (in some business, trade, or profession of his own) does not get a tax deduction for some entertainment-related expenditure, a hobby business owner's customer base could suffer. This occurs in those businesses which pitch to the customer's tax benefits rather than, or in addition to, his personal benefits.

Some recreational-type businesses (livelihood as well as hobby types) try to promote their business by advertising it as a legitimate tax deduction for business customers and their families. This is particularly true of convention sponsors, cruise ship outings, travel tours, sporting events, and theatrical performances with business and charitable overtones. Our position is: DO NOT MISLEAD your customers in this manner. You don't know; you have no way of knowing; nor should you even care to know, whether a customer gets a tax deduction for any money that he or she pays to you.

Perhaps 2% or so of your customers may indeed get a business expense deduction on their tax returns, for certain payments made to you. But this leaves 98% who get no such deduction. Therefore, level with your customers up front. In your advertising and promotional literature, make no mention whatsoever of any potential tax benefits to your customers. Instead, focus their attention on the pure personal pleasure and recreation that they derive from your products or services.

When a hobby business owner's tax return is examined, one item that is sure to be asked for is a copy of his "sales literature": catalog, brochure, or other advertisement.

The IRS examines "sales pitch" documents with three purposes in mind. One, it wants to assure itself that the nature of your hobby business is indeed bona fide: that it is not a sham. Two, it wants to assess whether your pitch is more tax motivated than user motivated. And, three, it wants to identify a source of customers (taxpayers) whom it can canvas for subsequent revenue goals. Besides you, the IRS is always looking for others whom it can tax nab. Unwittingly, your promotional literature can trap you, as well as some of your customers, into the IRS's obsession to disallow.

Our point is: Don't oversell what you don't have and can't do. And don't even hint at any potential tax benefits to your customers. We condense and present these "pearls of wisdom" in Figure 10.2.

Sports Related Businesses

The big time professional sports activities covered by national TV (baseball, basketball, football, ice hockey, etc.) are unlikely opportunities for hobby business participants. We add: *highly* unlikely. The owners of professional teams contract out all possible spin-off business through franchises and concessions. Their top athletes are millionaires. The testimonials of these athletes are sought by major corporations who advertise their products worldwide. This leaves the hobby entrepreneurial domain to local sporting activities only.

By "local sporting" we mean such activities as auto racing, sky diving, bungi jumping, white water rafting, ballooning, parasailing, water skiing, amateur golf tournaments, fishing boat chartering, and the like. Most of these local activities fit nicely into a hobby business owner's available time: weekends and vacations. To

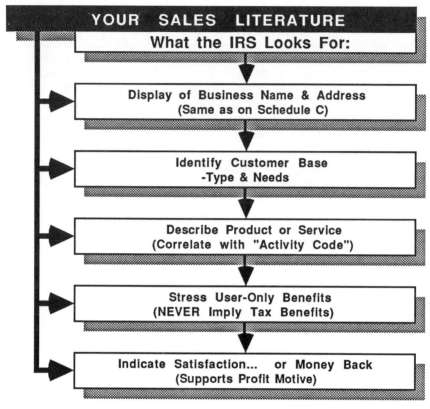

Fig. 10.2 - Pointers on Hobby Business Sales Literature

convince you that these activities can be tax successful, we'll cite a few recent decisions where the hobby sports venturer prevailed over the IRS.

Parasailing — An office supply salesman [*M.A. Stephens*, TC Memo 1991-383] engaged in a parasailing venture with the objective of making a profit. The court acknowledged that—

The taxpayer ran the parasailing operation in a businesslike manner, promoted his business through advertising, and maintained an accounting system to record receipts and disbursements.

Golf Tournaments — A school teacher [*D.C. Kimbrough*, TC Memo 1987-193] was allowed to deduct the losses he incurred in golfing activity which he pursued with the intention of making a profit. The court was persuaded that—

The taxpayer carefully detailed the expenses incurred for each tournament and recorded the tournament's available prize money, attended a business course for golfers, and spent significant amounts of time practicing both golf techniques and teaching methods. He also worked as an assistant golf pro. Although the taxpayer sustained losses for the years at issue, his earnings from golf increased steadily each year and gaining a tax advantage was not a substantial motivation.

Sailboat Chartering — A taxpayer [*D.A. Pryor*, TC Memo 1991-109] operated a sailboat chartering activity with a profit motive. The court allowed that—

The taxpayer carried on his boat charter activity in a businesslike manner, maintained separate bank account and records, conducted a study of anticipated revenues and expenses before entering into such activity, anticipated an increase in residual value of the sailboats, and employed competent and qualified managers.

Motorcycle Racing — An individual [*W. Canale*, TC Memo 1989-619] was allowed a deduction for his motorcycle racing expenses because he engaged in the activity with a profit objective. Among the factors the court considered were—

(1) There was a practical possibility that he could win enough money to exceed his expenses due to sufficiently large purses;
(2) The history of the taxpayer's racing activity was consistent with a desire to make a profit; and
(3) The taxpayer quit racing when he learned he could not compete on the professional level.

Hundreds (thousands) of hobby businesses in the local sporting arena run their activities with the intention of making a profit. Many do so as a by-product of their regular livelihood businesses. Relevant livelihood experience is a good qualifying prelude to hobby entrepreneurship.

Travel Related Businesses

Travel-related activities offer greater opportunities for hobby entrepreneurship than local sporting events. The whole world is at your fingertips (photographically speaking). One can be an independent tour guide, a free lance photographer, a travel writer for newspapers and magazines, a treasure hunter, a slide or video travel lecturer, a part-time travel agent, an inventor of travel accessories, and so on. To be tax successful, expertise and foreknowledge in a particular travel destination is required.

Most travel-related hobby businesses are summarily disallowed. The principal reason is Section 274(m)(1). It comes down hard on free-lance travel businesses because of the overriding implication of self-education. The subsection says very emphatically that—

No deduction shall be allowed . . . for expenses for travel as a form of education.

Travel-related hobby businesses tax fail because the elements of personal pleasure and education come through loud and strong. The entrepreneurs are too inattentive to businesslike activities and are often off to explore other travel sites before mastering their marketable skills and products. Some disallowance examples of what we mean follow.

Lecturer — The taxpayer was disallowed his travel expenses because: "He was not engaged in the business of lecturing on big game hunting adventure films with the intent to earn a profit." [*M.C. McGowan*, CA-7, 65-2 USTC 9516, 347 F2d 728.]

Photography — The taxpayer failed to prove that travel photography constituted an activity engaged in for profit. [*M.A. Stephens*, TC Memo 1991-383.]

Resort — Expenses for a vacation island owned by a physician were not deductible because of lack of profit motive. He did not apply for a commercial resort license; did not conduct promotional activities; and failed to maintain separate records for the business. [*J.B. Monfore*, Ct Cls, 77-1 USTC 9254.]

Treasure Hunting — The taxpayer was disallowed his travel and exploration expenses related to treasure-hunting activities because no income was ever produced. No business records were kept and the amount of time spent on the activity was negligible; the activity appeared to be primarily for recreational purposes. [*W.J. Hezel*, TC Memo 1985-10.]

Still, in an unpublished case, the IRS allowed all travel, lecturing, photography, and home office expenses for a college professor (who was a historian and archaeologist). On each vacation and each sabbatical, she traveled to established fossilized amber sites in Russia, the Baltic Region, the Middle East, Dominican Republic, Australia, and other countries. She was a paid lecturer and consultant at universities and museums worldwide. She wrote many scientific papers and was a recognized authority on the paleontology of amber.

Theatrics Related Businesses

In the world of entertainment, there are thousands of professional actors, singers, dancers, musicians, comedians, magicians, and others. Their talents and services are promoted and sponsored by professional agents and corporate producers. These are livelihood theatric activities which are outside the scope of our discussion.

There are, however, various hobby business opportunities for "wannabe" entertainers. These are amateur actors, singers, and dancers who participate in talent shows where money and prizes are at stake. There also are part-time musicians, comedians, magicians, jugglers, and high-wire acrobats who perform at scheduled events for stipend pay and barter exchanges. Most of these theatric persons require flashy wardrobes, uniforms, instruments, special equipment, and transportation to and from distant engagement sites. This is exactly the way that most established entertainers got their start in professional life. But the IRS — and the courts — don't always see it this way.

In the tax world, theatric hobby businesses are more frequently disallowed than allowed. Why? Because Regulation 1.274-2: Disallowance . . . for Entertainment, says so. It subregulation (b)(1) defines "entertainment" as—

Any activity which is of a type generally considered to constitute entertainment, amusement, or recreation . . . at night cubs, cocktail lounges, theaters, country clubs, athletic events, fashion shows, vacation trips . . . or similar [affairs].

Yet, in the case of *J.M. Green* [TC Memo 1989-599], it was held that the taxpayer's attempt to pursue an acting career was an activity carried on for profit. The court reasoned that—

The taxpayer spent a considerable amount of time on the activity, his efforts to secure acting parts were consistent with a profit motive, and his net income from acting in subsequent years dramatically increased.

Hobby theatric cases involving musical accompaniment, as a class, tend to be more tax successful than performers without music. The following three cases illustrate this pattern quite clearly:

• *B.D. Wagner* [TC Memo 1983-606] — The taxpayer made strong effort to promote his music by hiring a band, getting it booked, and hiring a singer with a "potential to draw sizable audiences."

• *L.F. Suiter* [TC Memo 1990-447] — The taxpayer was engaged in the business of performing country and western music for profit. He devoted considerable time to the activity and his losses were attributable to high car expenses and depreciation. The activity became profitable in years following the tax year in question.

• *D. Krebs* [TC Memo 1992-154] — A contemporary musical and theatrical promoter and his wife were allowed to take deductions on their joint return for the wife's music career because she spent considerable time securing musical contracts, and the losses were not sustained beyond a reasonable period.

Most hobby theatric businesses require miles of vehicular travel, many changes of wardrobes, and an assortment of electronic musical instruments. All of these items cost money. If an activity can survive the profit motive test, then a special $10,000 depreciation allowance (Section 179) may apply. We say "may apply" because the Section 179 deduction applies only if the net taxable income of one's **combined** hobby and livelihood activities equals or exceeds $10,000. A tax deduction of this amount provides a good headstart in recouping a theatric venturer's initial capital outlays.

Net Losses: Bottom Line

As stated previously, all hobby businesses of the type above require the filing of Schedule C (Form 1040). Where depreciation of vehicles, equipment, wardrobes, and instruments are allowed, Form 4562 is also required. If the depreciation allowance plus other operating expenses exceed your gross income from the business (for the filing year), your "bottom line" on Schedule C will be a net loss.

If this happens — and we expect that it will for several years, at least — the preprinted instructions on Schedule C say—

If you have a loss, you MUST check the box that describes your investment in this activity: ☐ *All investment is at risk.*
☐ *Some investment is not at risk.*

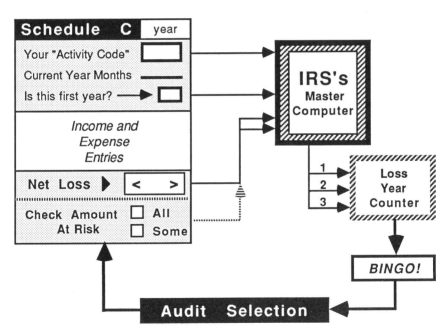

Fig. 10.3 - IRS's Computer Entrapment for Loss Years

If someone lends or gives you money without expecting its return, you are not "at risk" to that extent. Otherwise, if you borrow money and have to pay it back, or you "borrow" from your own savings, ALL of your investment is at risk. Therefore, be sure to check the "All" box.

There is also another check-box on Schedule C that you are to particularly note. It appears in the upper portion of the form and reads—

If this is the first Schedule C for this business check here ▸ ☐

We call this your "business starter" box. The IRS's computer scans this box for checking your profit motive under the rules of Section 183. If it is your starting year, and you have a net loss at the bottom of Schedule C, the IRS generally treats it as a "free year" for Section 183 purposes.

The following year you are asked (in the upper portion of Schedule C):

How many months was this business in operation during [the current year]? ▸ _____

If you enter less than 12 months, you also have to answer the question:

Was this business in operation at the end of [the current year]? ☐ *Yes* ☐ *No*

Don't you get it?

The IRS's computer is tracking your loss years and setting its disallowance trap. Maybe you'll "get it" better after glancing at Figure 10.3. After the second or third loss year, your return is automatically "red flagged" . . . for possible examination and audit.

11

CREATORS & COLLECTORS

Most Free Lance Artists, Photographers, Writers, And Collectors Use Their Home As Their Principal Place Of Business. This Requires Conformity To Section 280A(c) For Deductibility Of "Allocable" Expenses. Section 263A: Cost Capitalization, Is Harsh And Contentious. Fortunately, Exemptions Apply For QUALIFIED CREATIVE EXPENSES And Collections For Resale Of Less Than Ten Million Dollars. When Marketing Creative Or Collectible Items, Proper INVENTORY Is A "Must." Dollar-Costed Beginning And Ending Inventories Are Required. Your Allowable Tax Deductions Include All "Ordinary And Necessary" Expenses That Conform To Section 183 Relating To Losses.

In the world of small, small businesses, there is a class of hobby entrepreneurs which we characterize as creators and collectors. The "creators" are those who themselves create a marketable product with "their own hands and minds." Once a master original is created, multiple units are produced (by others than the creator) and offered for sale to the general public.

For our purposes, creators are free-lance artists, painters, sculptors, writers, poets, photographers, video filmers, restorers (of antiques), model makers, carvers, knitters, and the like These persons think up the product idea, do whatever research they have to, then produce the first reproducible copy. In practically every case, the work is done at home at all hours of the day or night. Economic necessity requires this, plus the fact that working at home does provide more time and solitude for creative endeavors. Most creative-type venturers have to have some livelihood business to sustain them.

Collectors, on the other hand, collect the creative works of others. They have a keen mind for selecting quality items and have a good marketing sense. They seek to collect "one of a kind" — an original if possible, but, if not, an authenticated copy of a "limited edition" production. They gather and mount related-era items into a limited number of marketable sets. The artistry and rarity of the items is where the profit potential lies. Collectors collect stamps, coins, guns, antiques, arrow heads, barbed wire, old books, old cars, rare paintings, genealogical artifacts, paper weights, toy soldiers, dolls, hunting trophies, etc., etc. Collectors, like creators, most often work at home.

Creators and collectors have special tax-bias problems. These are *inventory problems*: accounting and valuation. This is a tax domain where the IRS — which creates nothing but agony for others — can twist things around and "skew your books." By this tactic, many creators and collectors are forced into a positive income mode, whereas otherwise they would have a tax loss. It is for this reason that we focus this chapter on the inventory practices and home office rules that precede the application of Section 183.

Two Major Hurdles

When we gave you an overview of Section 183 back in Chapter 2, we did not raise a particular point that we now want to address. The point is embedded in Section 183(b)(1): Deductions Allowable. In a back-handed manner, this subsection reads—

In the case of an activity not engaged in for profit to which subsection (a) applies, there shall be allowed—

(1) the deductions which would be allowable under this [Tax Code] *for the taxable year without regard to whether or not such activity is engaged in for profit.*

Interpreted, this means that one has to comply with other applicable sections of the tax code first, **before** applying the rules of Section 183. If your expenses are allowable under other sections of the code, you are not home free. All it means is that you have passed some preliminary hurdles. And if you do not pass the preliminary hurdles, you do not even get to Section 183.

For creators and collectors, there are two particular hurdles which are quite major. Hurdle 1 is the business-use-of-home rule: Section 280A. Hurdle 2 is the capitalization and inventory rule: Section 263A. At the moment, all we want to do is to cite the titles and the nature of each rule. We'll expand on each one later.

Section 280A is captioned (in relevant part): *Disallowance of Certain Expenses in Connection With Business Use of Home, Etc.* Here we see that word "Disallowance" again. The substance of subsection (a) is—

> *Except as otherwise provided in this section, . . . no deduction otherwise allowable . . . shall be allowed with respect to the use of a dwelling unit which is used by the taxpayer . . . as a residence.*

This seems pretty clear: working at home, no deduction. We'll come back shortly to the "except as otherwise provided."

Section 263A is captioned: *Capitalization and Inclusion in Inventory Costs of Certain Expenses.* The substance of its subsection (a) is—

> *(1)   (A) In the case of property which is inventory in the hands of the taxpayer, shall be included in inventory, and*
> *(B) In the case of any other property shall be capitalized.*
> *(2)   (A) The allocable costs . . . with respect to any property are the direct costs of such property, and*
> *(B) such property's proper share of those indirect costs . . . which are allocable to such property.*

As you'll see shortly, Section 263A targets (1) property produced by taxpayers (creators), and (2) property acquired for resale (collectors). This section tries to "lock up" allocable costs in such a way that you get no deduction for your expenditures until the property is either sold or destroyed.

More On Section 280A

The above clause in Section 280A about "except as otherwise provided" is especially significant for creators and collectors. As hobby entrepreneurs, home is their principal place of business.

HOBBY BUSINESS VENTURES

Rarely is it otherwise. As such, subsection (c) of 280A provides an exception to the general "no deduction" rule.

Subsection 280A(c)(1): *Exception for Certain Business Use*, reads in full as—

Subsection (a) shall not apply to any item to the extent such item is allocable to a portion of the dwelling unit which is exclusively used on a regular basis—

*(A) as the **principal place of business** for any trade or business of the taxpayer,*

(B) as a place of business which is used by patients, clients, or customers in meeting or dealing with the taxpayer in the normal course of his trade or business, or

(C) in the case of a separate structure which is not attached to the dwelling unit, in connection with the taxpayer's trade or business. [Emphasis added.]

There are two key tests for your home expense deductions. One, a hobby venturer's home must be his principal place of business . . . for his hobby business. Two, there must be a designated (walled off) space which is exclusively used as an office, workshop, or studio. This second test is not difficult to meet as long as you measure off your business space and compute its fractional percentage of the total living area of your home. It is the "principal place" test that some hobbyists fail to meet.

One's principal place of (hobby) business is where he spends most of his time creating and collecting his marketable products. The amount of time spent at point of sale is also taken into consideration. The products may be sold by the creator/collector himself; they may be sold by others; they may be sold through the mail; or they may be sold at temporary sites set up and manned by agents for the creator/collector.

Regulation 1.280A-2(b)(3) addresses the issue of: *Determination of principal place of business*. We quote this subregulation to you in full. It reads—

When a taxpayer engages in a single trade or business at more than one location, it is necessary to determine the taxpayer's principal place of business for that trade or business in the light of all the facts and circumstances. Among the facts and circumstances to be taken into account in making this determination are the following:

(i) The portion of total income from the business which is attributable to the activities at each location;
(ii) The amount of time spent in the activities related to that business at each location; and
(iii) The facilities available to the taxpayer at each location for purposes of that business.

The idea is to take all relevant factors into consideration, then make a judgment call. Weigh such factors as time spent, money earned, facilities used, and other matters that we depict in Figure 11.1. It is much better that **you** make the judgment call rather than relying on the IRS to do it for you.

Once you decide that you qualify under Section 280A(c), you "stake your claim" to this effect by filing **Form 8829**: Expenses for Business Use of Home. Follow the instructions to said form and claim such items as a prorata portion of your property taxes, mortgage interest, casualty insurance, telephone, utilities, cleaning, maintenance, repairs, and so on.

More on Section 263A

Section 263A is one of the most obnoxious tax laws ever written. It was instigated in 1986 by the IRS as a gift to Congress for increasing the IRS's enforcement staff. It is a masterful way for raising revenue (which Congress likes) without raising taxes (which Congress dislikes).

Section 263A consists of nine primary subsections totaling about 4,500 words. Its regulations which the IRS prepared — get this — comprise OVER 36,000 WORDS! The whole idea is to force those large corporations who are allegedly not "paying their fair share," to capitalize certain "allocable" everyday operating expenses. This shifts many customary expenses which are ordinarily deductible currently into inventory and nondepreciable assets where said expenditures become "locked up" capital. The current-year income taxes are increased correspondingly.

There followed a lot of complaints to Congress from many thousands of small businesses about the burden of the IRS regulations. Congress responded by adding an exception to Section 263A for creators, and a separate exception for collectors. The exception for collectors is quite straightforward, so we'll tell you of it first.

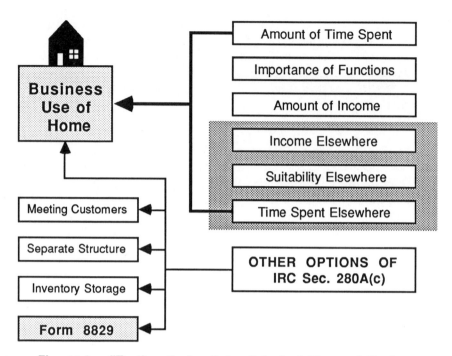

Fig. 11.1 - "Testing Factors" for Principal Place of Business

As we defined above, a hobby business "collector" is one who acquires creative property for resale. Subsection (b)(2)(B) of Section 263A provides an exception for taxpayers with gross receipts of $10,000,000 (10 million) or less. We doubt that any hobby business collector — in his wildest dreams — would ever achieve this volume of gross sales.

For your defensive reference, the step-sequence for identifying this exception is as follows:

Sec. 263A	— Capitalization and Inclusion in Inventory
Subsec. (b)	— Property for which Section Applies
Sub-subsec. (2)	— Property Acquired for Resale
Subsub-subsec. (B)	— EXCEPTION FOR TAXPAYER WITH GROSS RECEIPTS OF $10,000,000 OR LESS

Note that this exception for "property acquired for resale" is buried in the fourth level of tax law. Tax agents in the IRS rarely read beyond the first heading in a tax law. Consequently, if you want to claim the exception, you have to be knowledgeable enough to know where it exists, and you have to insist that the IRS read it.

Qualified Creative Expenses

The capitalization/inventorying harshness of Section 263A is softened, somewhat, for what is called: *Qualified creative expense.* This term is defined in subsection 263A(h)(2) as—

Any expense which is paid or incurred by an individual in the trade or business of such individual (other than as an employee) of being a writer, photographer, or artist, and . . . which, without regard to this section, would be allowable as a deduction for the taxable year. Such term does not include any expense related to printing, photographic plates, motion picture films, video tapes, or similar items.

Beyond the above, there is no regulation which describes in more detail exactly what constitutes a "creative expense." When a regulation is silent on a matter such a this, one has to refer to other portions of the tax code which use one or more similar phrases. In the creative expense case, the cross-referencing phrase is "trade or business" expense. This is the very title of Section 162: Trade or Business Expense. Its subsection (a) says—

*There shall be allowed as a deduction all the **ordinary and necessary** expenses paid or incurred . . . in carrying on any trade or business* [of the taxpayer]. [Emphasis added.]

There has been a lot of Tax Court litigation over defining the phrase "ordinary and necessary." The consensus seems to be that the term "ordinary" is that which is common and acceptable (even though infrequent) in the taxpayer's business. The term "necessary" is that which is appropriate and helpful to the business. Deductible expenses must be **both** ordinary and necessary. If ordinary but not necessary, or if necessary but not ordinary, the IRS will arbitrarily disallow the expenditure. This is the hardnosed stance that it takes when a particular expense item is beyond its own experience and comprehension. How many IRS agents really know when an expense is ordinary and necessary in the creative domain?

Section 263A(h)(1) says flat out that—

Nothing in this section [263A] *shall require the capitalization of any qualified creative expense.*

This subsection (h) is captioned: ***Exemption for Free Lance Authors, Photographers, and Artists.*** In other words, Section 263A does not apply to those expenses necessary for the creation of an original item. The exemption does *not* apply to subsequently produced multiple items. This IS the significance of the above statutory sentence which says—

Such term [qualified creative expense] *does not include any expense related to printing, photographic plates, motion picture films, video tapes, or similar items.*

Note the plurals in this sentence. Do not the terms printing plates, films, tapes, or items imply multiple reproductions of an original? Once a reproduction stage is undertaken, the capitalization and inclusion in inventory rules apply.

To help you visualize where creative expenses cease and Section 263A type costs begin, we present Figure 11.2. In this figure, we also indicate the kind of creative expenses that we believe are ordinary and necessary for writers, photographers, and artists.

Need for Inventories

Where there is a prospect of commercially marketing an item, the need for inventories arises. In its customary usage, the term "inventory" refers to any form of goods or merchandise held for sale in the ordinary course of one's trade or business. The goods or merchandise may be manufactured (created) for sale, or may be purchased (collected) for resale. Thus, if an item created or collected is not intended for sale, it is not inventory in the tax sense. Obviously, therefore, a free-lance writer or collector must have more than one or two items for sale in mind, in order to constitute a qualified hobby business.

Once the buildup of an inventory is envisioned, there arises the need for proper accounting thereof. Some common sense — not much — is permitted in this regard by Section 471(a) of the Internal

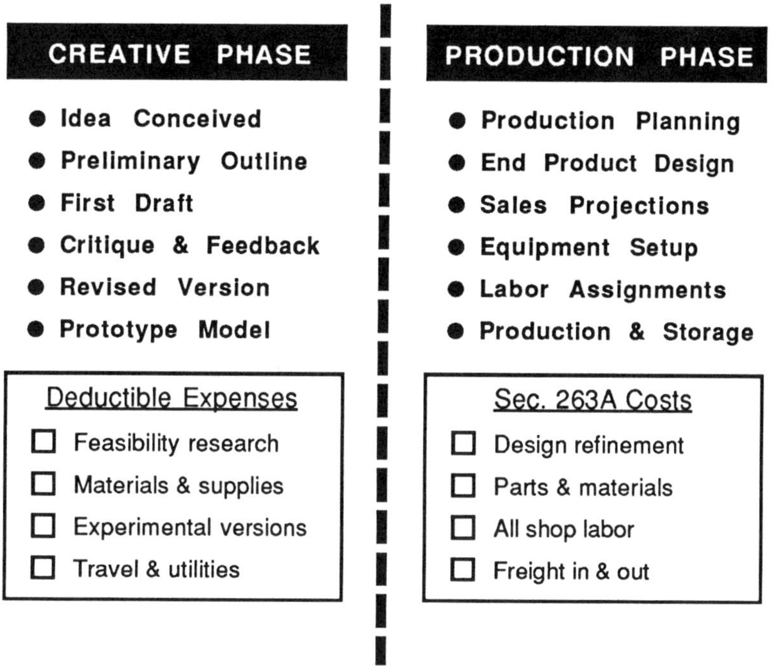

CREATIVE PHASE	PRODUCTION PHASE
● Idea Conceived	● Production Planning
● Preliminary Outline	● End Product Design
● First Draft	● Sales Projections
● Critique & Feedback	● Equipment Setup
● Revised Version	● Labor Assignments
● Prototype Model	● Production & Storage

Deductible Expenses	Sec. 263A Costs
☐ Feasibility research	☐ Design refinement
☐ Materials & supplies	☐ Parts & materials
☐ Experimental versions	☐ All shop labor
☐ Travel & utilities	☐ Freight in & out

Fig. 11.2 - The Creativity vs. Productivity "Dividing Line"

Revenue Code. This section, captioned: General Rule for Inventories, says, in essence, that a taxpayer may choose whatever accounting system he prefers, provided that it "most clearly reflects" his income. This means that inventories must be taken at the beginning and ending of each tax year in which the production, purchase, or sale of merchandise is an income-producing factor.

On this beginning/ending inventory note, Regulation 1.471-1: *Need for Inventories*, is quite helpful. It reads in pertinent part as—

The inventory should include all finished or partly finished goods and, in the case of raw materials and supplies, only those which have been acquired for sale or which will physically become a part of merchandise intended for sale. . . . Merchandise should be included in inventory only if title thereto is vested in the taxpayer. Accordingly, the seller should include in his inventory goods under contract for sale but not yet segregated and applied to the contract, and goods out upon consignment. A purchaser should include in inventory merchandise purchased (including containers), title to which has passed to him, . . . but should not include goods ordered for future delivery, transfer of title to which has not yet been effected. [Emphasis added.]

The "effecting" of title to goods, materials, supplies, and merchandise is often a tricky legal affair. It involves the legal enforceability of sell/buy contracts, physical control, and ownership rights during transit. We try to summarize and simplify for you in Figure 11.3 the above inventorying and titling concepts.

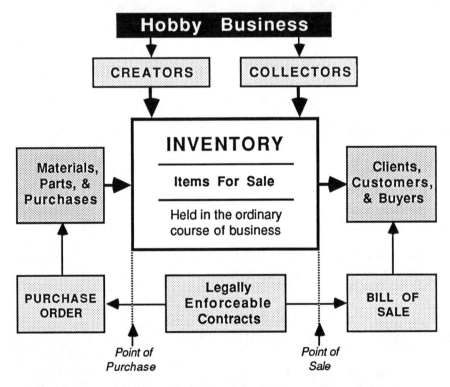

Fig. 11.3 - The Schematic Aspects of Inventory Ownership

"Cost of Goods Sold" Accounting

For tax accounting purposes, valuing an inventory becomes a special problem for creators and collectors. That special problem is: How do you value inventory where the personal efforts of its owner constitute the major and predominant role in its production or acquisition?

Answer: Don't ask the IRS to give you any help. Instead, follow Regulation 1.471-1 the best you can . . . and use common sense. Be cognizant of the fact that for inventory purposes only, your own personal labor carries no value whatsoever. True, your personal efforts are valuable to a buyer, but they cost you nothing out of your own pocket. Inventory "value" is that amount of money (or money equivalent) that you pay to someone else: **not** to yourself.

Basically, you value free-lance inventory by your direct out-of-pocket costs paid or incurred. Anything that you buy — materials, supplies, containers, parts, semi-finished goods, etc. — that goes into the goods or merchandise that you ultimately sell to customers and clients constitutes the cost value of your inventory. This is where the tax concept of "cost of goods sold" arises. Whatever it cost you — on a per unit basis — is your cost value on whatever you sell.

In a simplified computational way, the cost of goods sold affects your income accounting in the following manner:

Step 1 — Gross receipts from sales $_____
Step 2 — Opening inventory $_____
Step 3 — Closing inventory   _____
Step 4 — Cost of goods sold   _____
         [Subtract step 3 from step 2]
Step 5 — Gross profit (before expenses) $_____
         [Subtract step 4 from step 3]

As a free-lancer (small hobby business owner), you should not make yourself a slave to the harshness and sophistication of those inventory accounting procedures that major corporations use. After all, as a small business creator and collector, you are supposed to be exempt from the entire 36,000-word regulatory mandate of Section 263A.

Advertising & Promotion

The IRS is going to extract a price from you for being exempt from any of its regulations. It wants to be convinced that you are really trying to sell your inventory — of whatever type or form it may be. The absence of an aggressive selling and marketing program implies that you are engaged in your creative/collective endeavors more for personal reasons than for bona fide business reasons.

There is one way to at least partially overcome the IRS's presumption of your guilt of personal enjoyment. This is to engage a (small) commercial advertising firm to prepare a flyer, pamphlet, or catalog on your created or collected items that are being offered for sale. For this, your initial outlay in money may be a little high compared to the income from your hobby business. But, it may save you much tax aggravation in the long run. Being prepared by a third party (not involved in a tax dispute), your advertisement or promotional literature would put forward your best profit-seeking message. It would be done more objectively than if you were to prepare it yourself. The IRS is always skeptical of self-prepared documents that purport to establish business intent.

Instruct your advertising writer to prepare your promotional message along the lines that we set down back in Figure 10.2. Prepare your literature as though you had already been in business for five or six years . . . with resounding success. Of course, you want the message to ring true. By the time the IRS gets around to looking at your sales literature (to deduce your business product(s) and motive), several years will have gone by.

Most commercially prepared sales literature is undated. This is an advantage on one hand, and a disadvantage on the other. The advantage is that for tax purposes, the business objective of your hobby undertakings remains the same, regardless of the date the initial advertisement was prepared. Consequently, an "old" flyer, pamphlet, or catalog will serve your tax purpose just as well as an up-to-date one.

To provide a degree of up-to-dateness to your hobby business activities, run a low-cost ad in a newspaper, newsletter, or newsmagazine that serves your local area. Do this once or twice a year. Save the ad clippings for your tax files. Your objective is to show a continuity of effort in promoting your business affairs. You really must do this if you have three or more loss years in a row.

All advertising and promotional expenses are fully deductible as *ordinary and necessary* for any type of business: not just creative and collective. Other such expenses are presented in Figure 11.4. We list and edit those which are preprinted on Schedule C (Form 1040): Profit or Loss from Business.

Sched. C (Form 1040)	PROFIT OR LOSS FROM BUSINESS		
Questions and checkboxes			
Part I Income			
Gross sales less cost of goods sold			
Part II Expenses			
Advertising (& promotion)		Rent: equip. & vehicles	
Auto & van		Rent: storage & other	
Commissions & fees		Repairs & maintenance	
Dues & publications		Small tools ($100 or less)	
Insurance (business only)		Supplies (general)	
Interest (business only)		Taxes & licenses	
Legal & professional		Telephone (business only)	
Meals & entertainment		Travel & lodging	
Office expense		Utilities (business only)	
Postage & UPS		OTHER (specify)	
Part III Cost of Goods Sold			
See Text			

Fig. 11.4 - Type of Expense Deductible on Schedule C (1040)

Extent of Deductions Allowable

Regardless of the type of hobby business that you're in, your deductible expenses in Figure 11.4 are never unlimited. This is so, even if you are a full, bona fide profit-seeking activity for which your net losses may be allowed.

Section 183(b): **Deductions Allowable**, generally limit your deductions to an amount equal to the gross income derived from your hobby business. For example, if you generated $3,650 in gross income, your deductions would be limited to this amount, even though your otherwise legitimate expenses are $8,500. Unless you can capitalize the $4,850 difference (8,500 - 3,650) as startup-type expenses, you lose the excess expenditures.

You may include in your gross income (for purposes of computing your allowable deductions under Section 183(b) any net capital gains (excess of capital gains over capital losses) that are attributable to your hobby business. Such gains could occur when selling some of your used-in-business assets which are **not** inventory. This is a form of "income bonus" prescribed by Regulation 1.183-1(b)(4): Rule for capital gains and losses.

To overcome the general limitation rule above, one has to meet the presumption-of-profit rule of Section 183(d): **Presumption**. As you recall from Chapter 2, it is presumed that you are engaged in your hobby business for profit, if your gross income exceeds your allowable expenses in any three out of five consecutive years (two out of seven in the case of horses). If you meet this presumption, you can have at least two net loss years. This means that your allowable Figure 11.4-type expenses *can exceed* your hobby business income for these loss years.

Note that we expressly use the term "allowable" expenses for the loss years. The two loss years are allowable only if the IRS does not rebut the statutory presumption. The actual tax law wording says—

> . . . *unless the Secretary* [of Treasury to whom the IRS reports] *establishes to the contrary* . . . [that Sec. 183(d) does not apply}.

Now, the "Nitty-Gritty"

In frontline practice, the IRS never establishes or rebuts anything. It simply says "No," and forces you to prove that it is wrong.

Much too often, the IRS simply ignores the presumptive intent of Congress. When it does so, you have to challenge the IRS and convince it — or the Tax Court — that you are indeed genuinely profit motivated. For this, we urge that you again review Chapters 3 and 4. The IRS will not read them, but you should.

Once you get past the not-for-profit challenge that the IRS sets up, are you "free and clear"? You may be . . . but only on a year by year basis. For each year that you are free and clear, you may deduct *all* of your legitimate expenses, whether they exceed your hobby business income or not.

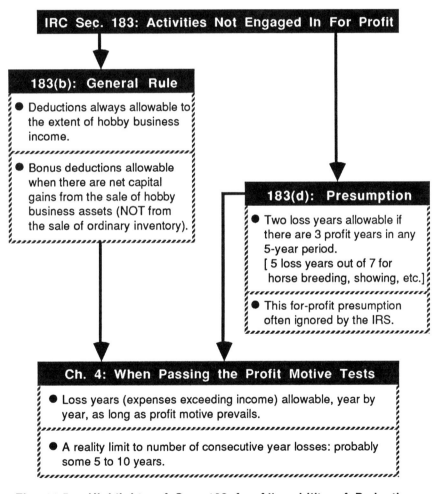

Fig. 11.5 - Highlights of Sec. 183 for Allowability of Deductions

But, at some point, reality sets in. How many years can you afford to run a hobby business at a loss, and still insist that you are profit motivated?

In our opinion, up to five consecutive loss years could be acceptable. Up to 10 loss years would be rarely acceptable. If over 10 consecutive loss years, do you really believe that anyone would conclude that you are truly profit motivated — and not tax motivated? Therefore, there comes a point in time, irrespective of what the IRS does or thinks, when one has to cease altogether his loss hobby business.

After a period of critiquing your loss experiences and exploring new venture potentials, you may decide to start a new hobby business in an entirely different field. If you decide to restart, Figure 11.5 could be a helpful refresher to you on the deduction highlights of Section 183.

If you do start another hobby business, our suggestion is: Wait one or two years. Better yet: Wait **three** years. It takes up to three years after a return is filed (if filed on time) to "wring it through" the IRS's computer watchdog system.

If you start a new loss venture within three years of abandoning your old one, it will be treated as an extension of your former activities. Using its sovereign authority, the IRS will assert: "You're trying to get away with something." It will point out that, by abandoning your previous venture, you have admitted that it was not for profit. Consequently, restarting too soon implies that you are carrying forward the same nonprofit intent.

12

CONTESTING DISALLOWANCES

As A Section 183 Venturer, There Will Come A Time When You Will Be Notified To Bring "Complete Records" Into Your Local IRS Office For Examining Selected Items On Your Return(s). Most, If Not All, Of Your Hobby Business Expenses And Deductions Will Be Disallowed. You Can Contest Any Or All Disallowances By [1] Indicating So To The Auditor, [2] Appealing Within The IRS (Regional Office Of Appeals), And [3] Petitioning The U.S. Tax Court. When Contesting, You Must Cite The ERRORS IN FACT And ERRORS IN LAW That Were Made By The IRS. The Experience Of These Contestations Can Be Beneficial To You In The Future.

In each of chapters 6 through 11 previously, we presented different examples of everyday, hobby-type businesses. We exemplified the tax forms and backup documentation needed. We also indicated the kind of attitude and "business front" that you should maintain. Our underlying thesis of each example was that the venture, while losing money initially, had the potential of turning profitable at some point in downstream time.

In this closing chapter, we want to bring tax reality closer to home. Sooner or later, any nonlivelihood business, which the IRS classifies as such, will trigger some kind of computer notification to you. The notification may be a routine computer mismatching assertion (you didn't report all of your income), or an arithmetic correction (because you didn't use the proper forms or enter on the correct lines). The notification may also be a *Selection for Examination* (audit). In such a case, there are certain "look back" features that you have to worry about. The IRS is the greatest wonder of the world in hindsight: never in foresight.

When you are selected for what is called a "Section 183 audit," it is almost a guarantee that your hobby losses will be disallowed arbitrarily. This is routine procedure. By automatically saying "No," the IRS forces the taxpayer to prove that he or she was correct when claiming the losses. Consequently, if you do not contest the automatic disallowance, the disallowance automatically stands. In this chapter, we want to give you some pointers and guidance for contesting — and overcoming — the disallowance of your hobby business losses.

Form of Selection Notice

Don't be alarmed. Be forewarned and get prepared. Get prepared to stand up to the IRS and test your mettle. This also means testing your records and expertise.

One of these days (if you haven't already) you'll receive a brown, window-type, letter-size envelope, with the sender's address in bold print—

> Department of Treasury
> Internal Revenue Service
> District Director ____(city)____

We assure you that this envelope will contain no refund check. Nor will it contain any headnote for quick identity of what it is. There is no courtesy salutation of any kind.

The "letter" starts off brusquely—

> *Your Federal income tax return has been selected for examination. On the reverse side please see the specific items to be examined for the tax year(s) shown below. It is very important that you contact our office **within 10 days** from the date of this letter.* [Emphasis added.]

Thus, within 10 days, you've got to do something. But don't panic. You don't have to produce your records within 10 days. All you have to do is make a phone call . . . *to arrange an appointment.*

The telephone number of the appointment clerk appears at the upper right-hand corner of the notification letter.

At the minimum, make your audit appointment at least 30 days away. In no case, make it more than 90 days away. You are going to have to face the music, so get ready by knuckling down. Go through your records and start getting them organized. By the date on your notice, your Section 183 records will be **more than** 18 months old — could be as much as three to five years old. Obviously, you need a reasonable amount of time to get ready. Most IRS appointment clerks try to be accommodating.

On the reverse side of your notification letter or an on attachment to it, you will find a directive which starts out with—

Please bring records to support the following items reported on your tax return for [_year(s)_].

The general format and contents of this directive are along the lines presented in Figure 12.1.

As you can see in Figure 12.1, your audit notification contains a lot of check-boxes. Some have preprinted items alongside; other check-boxes do not. The blank check-boxes are obviously intended for special hand entries by the IRS auditor or agent who is going to conduct the exam. If a box is not hand-checked (usually with an X or √), you can ignore that item . . . at least for your initial interview. You do **not** have to dig up every item preprinted on the audit notification form.

Your notification letter goes on to say—

Please bring this letter with you to the interview. Also bring the **complete records** *needed to verify the items checked. Without the requested records, we will have to* **proceed on the basis of** *available information.* [Emphasis added.]

That phrase about proceeding on the basis of "available information" is grossly misleading. It is bureaucratese for saying—

"If you don't provide the records requested, we will disallow ALL expenses and deductions on the items we have checked."

Again, we remind you: arbitrary disallowance — especially of Section 183 matters — is "standard procedure." The IRS is not

---

INTERNAL REVENUE SERVICE	District Director

[Person to Contact]

[Phone No. & Date]

[Tax Year(s) Selected]

● **Your return(s) ... selected for examination.**

> **Appointment Information**
> ● Place _____ ● Date _____
> ● Room _____ ● Time _____

● **Bring this letter and COMPLETE RECORDS for items checked -**

General

☐ Emplyee expenses   ☐ Cap. gains/losses   ☐)
☐ Casualty losses   ☐ Rents/royalties   ☐) Other
☐ Auto expenses   ☐ Rental expenses   ☐)

Schedule C

☐ Gross receipts   ☐ Car & truck   ☐)
☐ Cost of goods   ☐ Legal expenses   ☐) Other
☐ Depreciation   ☐ Travel expenses   ☐)

Schedule F

☐ Gross receipts   ☐ Machine hire   ☐)
☐ All expenses   ☐ Insurance   ☐) Other
☐ Depreciation   ☐ Repairs/supplies   ☐)

Fig. 12.1 - General Contents of Selection Notice for Office Audit

about to go out of its way to help you save taxes. All such effort must be expended by you.

Prepare "Relevant Factors" Statement

Back in Chapter 4: Profit Motive Criteria, we described the nine relevant factors which the IRS uses to determine if your hobby business expenses should be allowed. These factors/tests derive from Regulation 1.183-2(b)(1) through (9). At this point, we urge that you go back and quickly review that chapter. Then prepare your own statement of applicable facts.

Strictly in preliminary form, prepare your own statement in the third-person sense. You want the statement to sound impersonal and authoritative. You really want to demonstrate your knowledge and expertise in your chosen hobby business venture.

For example, suppose your nonlivelihood activity was cattle breeding and selling calves. You have access to a large ranch, to which you go after your livelihood-work hours and on weekends. Suppose that you are addressing Factor 3: Time and Effort Expended. Here's a sample of what you might write:

"During the six-month period of September through February (the breeding/calving season), taxpayer spends two to three hours each day (after her regular work hours) attending the cattle. She drives a truck around a 900-acre ranch distributing hay, checking on cattle (which she branded herself), spraying them for worms, and vaccinating them against Lepto and Vibro (which are diseases causing abortion in cows). During the six-month period of March through August, she spends about 10 to 15 hours each weekend riding through her grazing herd, fixing fences, selecting calves for branding and carting, and vaccinating them for "black leg" and "red water" (a urine infection). She does this all on her own. This is hard work and no pleasure. Nor is there any sport or pleasure in gathering up the dead carcasses of diseased cows, calves, and prime bulls."

The idea is to prepare carefully and in detail a statement on all nine of the profit motive factors. You do this primarily for the purpose of getting yourself mentally prepared and psyched up. You have spent a lot of time, money, and effort trying to get your venture moving ahead. You are not going to let some behind-the-desk IRS person, with a revenue quota to meet, who has not tried his hand at a business venture of his own, beat you out of your legitimate deductions. You are just not going to let this happen.

But it will happen, unless you doggedly do your homework. Can you imagine any IRS person understanding Factor 3 above, without your explaining it in all the gory details?

Meaning of Complete Records

The audit notification letter that you receive expressly tells you to—

. . . bring the complete records needed to verify the items checked.

It is reasonable, therefore, for you to ask: What is meant by "complete" records?

As per IRC Section 7602(a): Examination of Books, the complete records phrase means—

. . . any books, papers, records, or other data which may be **relevant or material** *to such* [examination]. [Emphasis added.]

In other words, the records which you are expected to have are those which are necessary to substantiate and justify each and every questioned entry on your return. By "substantiate," we mean the *amount* that you entered; by "justify," we mean the *reason* for your entry.

Complete records certainly mean all those invoices, receipts, cancelled checks, books of account, mileage logs, appointment books, income sources, etc., etc. Your records include *anything and everything* that is **relevant or material** to the audit. There are no minimum standards: no maximum standards. Whatever you used to prepare your return, and whatever rationale you used to justify your entries, constitute your complete records.

For Section 183 (not-for-profit) activities, you'll particularly need some novel records. For example, reconsider Factor 3 above. Here's a case where it would be "relevant and material" to have a few photographs of the old ranch truck with two or three dead animal carcasses loaded on. Photographs of the taxpayer in her grungy clothes vaccinating the animals would be helpful. So, too, would articles clipped from farming journals on the feeding and care of prime bulls; articles and advertisements on market prices, auction houses, animal exchange (stud) services; medical articles on animal diseases; etc. "Novel" records are those which common sense tells you that you need for educating persons who are totally unknowledgeable in your hobby business affairs.

It's also a good idea to have two or three favorable court rulings by other taxpayers who have engaged in hobby businesses similar to yours. We gave you some ideas in this regard back in Chapter 3. But we gave only the digests. You want the complete, published findings of fact for the cases you intend to rely on. You'll probably need some assistance from a tax professional in selecting near-identical cases to yours.

Keep in mind that the whole idea behind the IRS's selecting your return for audit is to disallow your hobby business expenses. It is not to compliment you for your hard work, good records, and well-preparedness. No auditor is going to read all of your files and records; he'll pick and choose among them. But the fact that you have complete records available and ready will convey the message that you mean business . . . serious business.

Audit Change Report

Within from 30 to 180 days after appearing for audit, you'll receive a computer printout titled: *Report of Examination Changes*. The printout itself will consist of five to ten pages (single-sided), depending on the scope and depth of the audit exam. The printout will be accompanied by a cover letter and an attachment called "Publication 5." We'll defer, temporarily, any discussion of Publication 5.

The cover letter is two pages, front and back. It consists of about 750 words, and is arranged in eight paragraphs (unnumbered). It is dated and facsimile stamped with the name of the District Director of the IRS office where the exam was conducted.

Like all IRS correspondence to taxpayers, there is no quick-identity in the heading of the cover letter. You have to begin reading in order to figure out what they are talking about. The two-sentence opening paragraph reads—

*Enclosed are two copies of our report explaining why we believe **adjustments should be made** in the amount of your tax. Please look this over and let us know whether you agree with our findings.* [Emphasis added.]

Don't read beyond this opening paragraph. Instead, turn to the computer printout: pages 1 and 2 thereof. Above the blank space where the IRS obviously wants you to sign, there is an entry item marked: **Balance Due**. Our abbreviation of the computer printout is presented in Figure 12.2. If the balance due, plus penalties, is below your tolerance threshold — say, several hundred dollars or several thousand — you might as well agree and pay. Every taxpayer has his/her own threshold of tolerance for contesting tax

I R S	REPORT OF INDIVIDUAL INCOME TAX EXAMINATION CHANGES			Dept. of Treasury
Name / Address of Auditee	Audit Year	Filing Status		Audit Group
	Date of Report	Identifying Number		IRS District

INCOME AND DEDUCTION AMOUNTS ADJUSTED

Ref. No.	Item Changed	Amount Shown	Corrected Amount	Increase (Decrease)

TOTAL ADJUSTMENTS: INCREASE (DECREASE)➤

TAX COMPUTATIONS	
TAX CREDITS	
OTHER TAXES	
CORRECTED TAX ➤	
DEFICIENCY (Increase in tax)	
OVERASSESSMENT (Decrease in tax)	
PREPAYMENTS	
BALANCE DUE ➤	
REFUND ┄┄➤	
PENALTIES ➤	

Auditee's Consent and Signature Block

Fig. 12.2 - Edited Format of Office Audit Report

matters. We can't suggest what your standards might be. Disagreeing will test your patience, persistence, and fortitude.

If the "balance due" exceeds your tolerance threshold, go back to the cover letter. Read the third paragraph, which starts out as—

If you do not accept our findings, you have 30 days from the date of this letter to do one of the following:

1. Mail us additional evidence or information . . .
2. Request a discussion with the examiner . . .
3. Discuss your position with the group manager or a senior examiner . . .

Then, paragraph 7 (next to last) goes on to say—

*If we do not hear from you **within 30 days**, we will have to process your case on the basis of the adjustments shown in the examination report. . . .*

There you have it. You can either agree (and pay) or disagree (and not pay). You can also agree in part (and pay in part) or disagree in part. Whatever your disagreement is, your intention to that effect must be made known to the IRS within 30 days of the adjustment report. Because of this 30-day requirement, this communication is generally referred to as a "30-day" letter. Officially, it is **Letter 915**; unofficially, it is called a "preliminary report."

Object First to Auditor

Unless you have decided to quit your hobby business altogether, we think you should object and disagree with the initial findings. Do this with the purpose of gaining experience in the system. If you are going to continue your hobby business, or switch to another type, you'll face audit challenges many more times to come. You might as well grit your teeth and decide to challenge back.

The first contesting thing to do is to phone the examiner and leave the message that you disagree. Also state that you will submit the basis of your disagreement in writing, within the prescribed time. Don't discuss your disagreement over the phone; put it in writing. Don't even ask for a discussion with the group manager or a senior examiner. In 99% of the cases, these persons will support the initial auditor's position. It is the auditor who confronted you that you confront back.

Before preparing your disagreement letter, review the *Explanation of Adjustments* that accompanied the computer change printouts. Ostensibly, the IRS is supposed to explain why each and every adjustment was made to your return. The so-called "explanations" are stereotyped, bureaucratic, and almost totally meaningless. Typical examples are:

(a) *We have disallowed the amount shown on your return because you did not furnish the information needed to support the deduction claimed.*

(b) *With the information you provided, we have no alternative but to treat this as a business engaged in not-for-profit.*

(c) *It has been determined that the underpayment of tax is due to negligence or intentional disregard of rules and regulations.*

The only real virtue to these explanations is that they itemize the particular matters that were adjusted. You need to refer expressly to these same items when you prepare your written disagreement.

Address your disagreement letter to the same auditor who personally conducted the examination. Be forceful and factual about it. Be courteous, but do not grovel. Don't rant and rave about the tax system being unfair. Who ever said it was fair? Stick to the item or items disallowed, and why you disagree. Reference your letter to all the symbols, names, and years identified in the IRS's adjustment letter to you. Then add: DISAGREEMENT WITH, just below the official reference symbols at the upper right-hand portion of your letter.

Clearly State All Errors

The IRS makes a lot of errors in its administration of the tax laws. Some of these errors are just plain carelessness and arbitrariness on the IRS's part. Some of the errors are due to the mindset of bureaucracy. Some are due to its misreading and misinterpretation of applicable law. And some are due to the sport of intimidating taxpayers that the IRS enjoys.

Whatever your disagreement really is, you have to focus your attention on portraying each disagreement as an administrative ERROR. Every tax error has two components, namely:

(1) Error in **fact**, and
(2) Error in **law**.

If there is the slightest doubt in your mind about the appropriateness and propriety of an IRS adjustment to your return, challenge it as an error. It probably is.

For example, suppose you own a 25-year-old stable, barn, and corral complex where you shelter and feed ten dwarf one-humped Arabian camels (called: dromedaries). You bought the complex recently at a cost of $350,000. You paid $7,848 in plumbing and electrical repairs, which the auditor disallowed. He/she insisted that you capitalize the expenditures (add them to the $350,000), but you disagree.

In your disagreement letter, you cite the item and amount (Repairs $7,848) that the auditor disallowed. Then you prepare your statement of disagreement along the following lines:

[1: Error in Fact] You have erred in that the disallowed $7,848 were incidental repairs necessary to keep the property in operation for its intended purpose: the stabling and feeding of dwarf camels.

[2: Error in Law] You have erred in that you have misinterpreted Treas. Reg. 1.263(a)-1(b) which says that: *Amounts paid for incidental repairs and maintenance of property are not capital expenditures.* Compared to a $350,000 complex, plumbing and electrical repairs in the amount of $7,848 are truly "incidental." They will not "substantially prolong" the depreciable life of the complex.

And so on down the IRS's list of disallowed items. By citing your disagreement in terms of errors in fact AND (correspondingly) errors in law, you've put the IRS on notice that you have already done some homework. You imply that you have every intention of doing more homework. You may need some professional tax help in this regard. If so, insist that your counselor provide you with specific references — such as tax code sections, IRS regulations, revenue rulings, court rulings, etc. — that support your position. Then "hang in there" . . . for the long haul.

The Second Change Letter

Even though you have to respond to the IRS's "report of change" letter within 30 days, it is rare that the IRS will respond to your response in less than six months (180 days). It does have to respond, as otherwise its nonresponse would be tantamount to conceding its case. It is too eager for additional revenue to allow this to happen.

Often the response is a reaffirmation of the initial adjustment changes. Sometimes a token adjustment to the initial adjustment is made. In the disagreement example of $7,848 in repairs above, the IRS auditor agreed that one-half the amount ($3,924) was indeed repairs. But he held that the other one-half ($3,924) had to be treated as a capital item, depreciable over seven years. Once in a great while the IRS may accept your disagreement letter in full. In such case it will issue you a "no change" letter.

More likely, however, you'll get still another adjustment letter: your second one. This second change letter will repeat the previous disallowances that have not been changed. It will also show the reduced disallowances, if any.

The second adjustment letter will be somewhat similar to the first report of changes. This time, however, it contains more formality of tone. Its leadoff sentence will read as—

> *Thank you for the information you gave us about your Federal income tax liability for the above year. We considered it carefully* . . . [But] . . .
>
> ☐ *We did not change our previous determination for the reasons given on the enclosed form(s).*
>
> ☐ *We adjusted your tax liability as shown in the enclosed revised examination report.*
>
> *If you agree with our findings,* . . .
> *If you do not agree, you may* . . .

Now, what do you do?

Officially, this second change notice is designated as **Letter 692**. Unofficially, it is a 10-day final report notice. You have 10 days only to let the IRS know what you intend to do. Ten days, that's it.

This is where Publication 5, mentioned earlier, comes in handy. Pub. 5 is titled: *Appeal Rights and Preparation of Protests for Unagreed Cases*. It is a 2-page document in 3-columnar form. It comprises about 2,500 words. Its two major parts are—

A. Appeals Within the IRS, and
B. Appeals to the Courts.

Its explanation of your options is fairly clear, and we certainly urge that you do read it.

Start reading Pub. 5 at the paragraph which is headed—

If You Don't Agree

If you don't agree with the second change letter, you are told that you can appeal your case **within** the IRS. You do this by applying to the IRS's Regional Office of Appeals. Publication 5 and the second change letter tell you that—

> *If you wish a conference with the Regional Office of Appeals, you MUST LET US KNOW within 10 days. . . . An appeals officer, who has not examined your return previously, will review your case. The appeals office is independent of the district director and resolves most disputes informally and promptly. . . . An appeals officer will telephone you and arrange an appointment if necessary.* [Emphasis added.]

The regional Appeals Office is the only level of appeal within the IRS. The procedures are quite informal. Appeals are conducted mostly in writing and by telephone. Rarely is it necessary to appear in person at the regional office. Consequently, we urge that you engage fully in the appeals process, if you don't agree with the latest disallowance letter the IRS sent you.

Appeals Process Summarized

The appeals process involves three different monetary levels of unagreed/disputed amounts. These amounts (including penalties) are—

1. Not more than $2,500
2. More than $2,500 but not more than $10,000
3. More than $10,000

The procedural aspects at each level are summarized in Figure 12.3. Publication 5 and the latest IRS change letter encourage you to phone a designated Review Coordinator to discuss the local procedures.

There is a reason for the three monetary levels of procedure. Each level represents a different degree of *settlement authority*

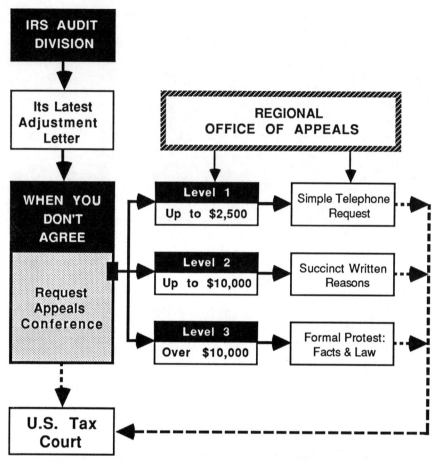

Fig. 12.3 - The Appeals Procedure Within the IRS

empowered to the appeals officer. For Level 1 ($2,500 or less), the appeals office can give a little more, if your position is reasonable and well founded. This usually involves your mailing some additional information which the disallowing auditor did not have.

For Level 2 ($10,000 or less), you need to write your reasons for disagreeing in succinct form. You must identify each unagreed adjustment in a *Statement of Disputed Issues*. The IRS will provide the format to you if you so request. Otherwise, it is along the lines as follows:

I disagree with your proposed adjustments and wish a conference with an appeals officer. The proposed adjustments to which I disagree, and my reasons for disagreement are as follows:

Unagreed Adjustments   Reason for Disagreement

(a) ....   (a) ....
(b) ....   (a) ....
(c) ....   (c) ....

_____/s/_____   _____
Your signature   Date

Your reason(s) should be crisp and well directed. For example, suppose that $5,118 of your computer parts and software were disallowed, for tracking the feeding/breeding/training of your dromedary camels. Your reason for disagreeing might read—

Miscellaneous computer parts, extension plugs, and special-use software (in the amount of $5,118) separately and irregularly purchased for use with $27,119 in computers and accessories (separately entered on depreciation schedules), plus other ordinary and necessary materials and supplies which you allowed truly constitute "supplies and small tools" as initially entered on the return. [Reg. 1.162-3 & Reg. 1.263(a)-1(b).]

At Level 2, if you present a factually strong case, the appeals officer may compromise some. If a negligence penalty has been added, he may even abate that portion altogether. At this level, he is dealing with "hazards of litigation." He is testing your smarts and willingness to go into Tax Court. Usually, there is a lot of writing, referencing (to Rules and Regulations), and phone calls back and forth. You never know where you stand until one day the appeals officer phones and says—

If we can close this case promptly, I propose the following—

. . . or words to this effect.

Closing a case doesn't mean that the IRS has conceded. It simply means that the IRS has given a little, and you are expected to give in, by accepting some disallowance.

Over $10,000: Formal Protest

Level 3 (over $10,000) involves more formality in the appeals procedure. You have to make a formal protest and sign it "under penalties of perjury." For the protest format, the IRS directs that you follow the instructions in Publication 5.

In essence, for Level 3 appeals, you prepare a document which you head as: PROTEST; UNAGREED MATTERS. The general format goes as follows—

Re: (a) Your name & SSN
(b) Symbols & date on IRS's letter
(c) Tax year(s)

1. Request is made for conference with the Appeals Office to discuss unagreed matters arising from examination of the income tax return(s) referenced above.

2. The unagreed matters for discussion are:
(a) ....   [Itemized listing of each disallowance
(b) ....   with which you disagree; its nature
(c) ....   and amount.]

3. The facts pertinent to this protest are:
(a) ....   [Chronological presentation of each
(b) ....   fact or set of facts addressing each
(c) ....   unagreed item above.]

4. The applicable law and its relevance to this protest are:
(a) ....   [Cite, as appropriate, pertinent sections
(b) ....   of the tax code, regulations, revenue
(c) ....   rulings, and legislative history of the
(x) ....   core tax law on which you rely.]

Respectfully submitted,

_____/s/_____
(your name/Taxpayer)

Under penalties of perjury, I declare that the facts presented in my written protest, which are set out above, are, to the best of my knowledge and belief, true, correct, and complete.

_____/s/_____ _(date)_
(your name/Taxpayer)

We have to be honest with you. A Level 3 appeal will probably not produce much in your favor. This is especially true of hobby business (Section 183) cases. The appeals officer's settlement authority is pretty well limited to those Section 183 issues on which the IRS has lost in court before. About the best he will do for you is a cleanup of any computational errors, back down (a little) on peripheral (non-core) issues, and modify any harsh judgment calls on depreciation class lives and methods.

Your protest appeal will be scrutinized by the Regional Director's legal staff. The idea is to see if the IRS wants to make a Tax Court "test case" out of your hobby undertakings. Or, to see if the IRS has already won on cases similar to yours. All of which means that you should only protest those matters on which you are willing to go to Tax Court.

End-of-Appeals Signal

At a Level 3 appeal, you'll experience much delay and procrastination by the appeals officer. Part of this is due to his many consultations with the IRS's legal staff. And part is due to his limited settlement authority. It is only in those situations where the IRS is **clearly erroneous** (which it seldom admits) that any concessions are made.

Without your realizing it, at some point in the appeals process, there will be a clear signal that you have reached the end of the line. In fairly blunt terms, you will be requested to sign one or both of these two forms, namely:

Form 866: Agreement as to Final Determination of Tax Liability

Form 872: Consent to Extend the Time to Assess Income Tax [OR, Form 872-A: Special Consent to Extend the Time to Assess Tax]

If you decline to sign either of these forms, the appeals officer will unilaterally close the case at his end. You will then be sent by certified mail a formal **Notice of Deficiency**. This is the IRS's way of cutting off the appeal and saying (in effect)—

Pay the amount disallowed within 90 days, OR petition the U.S. Tax Court for further consideration of your unagreed matters.

Depending on how strongly you feel about your hobby business activities, you may indeed want to try your hand at Tax Court proceedings. Many other hobby business venturers before you have done so. This is why we devoted Chapter 3 entirely to selected court rulings. We wanted you to recognize that if your unagreed issues are well focused and bona fide, you have at least a 50/50 chance of prevailing in court. The fact that the IRS cuts you off in its appeals process is no prognosis whatsoever of your outcome in Tax Court.

Going into Tax Court requires that the IRS issue you a formal **Notice of Deficiency**. This notice starts your statutory 90 days within which to file a Petition for Redetermination of the disallowances that the IRS has asserted against you. When receipted by the Tax Court, your petition sets in motion a whole new chain of adversarial stances between you and the IRS.

All along, our contention has been that, on hobby business matters, the IRS is not your friend. With this in mind, you might as well get your Section 183 contestation experiences up front. If you do — and you survive reasonably intact — you'll be in a much stronger position to survive subsequent tax attacks. In any side business endeavor, it is *experience* — both good and bad — that counts . . . for success.

ABOUT

THE AUTHOR

Holmes F. Crouch

Born on a small farm in southern Maryland, Holmes was graduated from the U.S. Coast Guard Academy with a Bachelor's Degree in Marine Engineering. While serving on active duty, he wrote many technical articles on maritime matters. After attaining the rank of Lieutenant Commander, he resigned to pursue a career as a nuclear engineer.

Continuing his education, he earned a Master's Degree in Nuclear Engineering from the University of California. He also authored two books on nuclear propulsion. As a result of the tax write-offs associated with writing these books, the IRS audited his returns. The IRS's handling of the audit procedure so annoyed Holmes that he undertook to become as knowledgeable as possible regarding tax procedures. He became a licensed private Tax Practitioner by passing an examination administered by the IRS. Having attained this credential, he started his own tax preparation and counseling business in 1972.

In the early years of his tax practice, he was a regular talk-show guest on San Francisco's KGO Radio responding to hundreds of phone-in tax questions from listeners. He was a much sought-after guest speaker at many business seminars and taxpayer meetings. He also provided counseling on special tax problems, such as divorce matters, property exchanges, timber harvesting, mining ventures, animal breeding, independent contractors, selling businesses, and offices-at-home. Over the past 20 years, he has prepared nearly 9,000 tax returns for individuals, estates, and small businesses.

During the tax season of January through April, he prepares returns in a unique manner. During a single meeting, he completes the return . . . *on the spot!* The client leaves with his return signed, sealed, and in a stamped envelope. His unique approach to preparing returns and his personal interest in his clients' tax affairs have honed his professional proficiency. His expertise extends through itemized deductions, computer-matching of income sources, capital gains and losses, business expenses and cost of goods, residential rental expenses, limited and general partnership activities, closely-held corporations, to family farms and ranches.

He remembers spending 12 straight hours completing a doctor's complex return. The next year, the doctor, having moved away, utilized a large accounting firm to prepare his return. Their accountant was so impressed by the manner in which the prior return was prepared that he recommended the doctor travel the 500 miles each year to have Holmes continue doing it.

He recalls preparing a return for an unemployed welder, for which he charged no fee. Two years later the welder came back and had his return prepared. He paid the regular fee . . . and then added a $300 tip.

During the off season, he represents clients at IRS audits and appeals. In one case a shoe salesman's audit was scheduled to last three hours. However, after examining Holmes' documentation it was concluded in 15 minutes with "no change" to his return. In another instance he went to an audit of a custom jeweler that the IRS dragged out for more than six hours. But, supported by Holmes' documentation, the client's return was accepted by the IRS with "no change."

Then there was the audit of a language translator that lasted two full days. The auditor scrutinized more than $1.25 million in gross receipts, all direct costs, and operating expenses. Even though all expensed items were documented and verified, the auditor decided that more than $23,000 of expenses ought to be listed as capital items for depreciation instead. If this had been enforced it would have resulted in a significant additional amount of tax. Holmes strongly disagreed and after many hours explanation got the amount reduced by more than 60% on behalf of his client.

He has dealt extensively with gift, death and trust tax returns. These preparations have involved him in the tax aspects of wills, estate planning, trustee duties, probate, marital and charitable bequests, gift and death exemptions, and property titling.

Although not an attorney, he prepares Petitions to the U.S. Tax Court for clients. He details the IRS errors and taxpayer facts by citing pertinent sections of tax law and regulations. In a recent case involving an attorney's ex-spouse, the IRS asserted a tax deficiency of $155,000. On behalf of his client, he petitioned the Tax Court and within six months the IRS conceded the case.

Over the years, Holmes has observed that the IRS is not the industrious, impartial, and competent federal agency that its official public imaging would have us believe.

He found that, at times, under the slightest pretext, the IRS has interpreted against a taxpayer in order to assess maximum penalties, and may even delay pending matters so as to increase interest due on additional taxes. He has confronted the IRS in his own behalf on five separate occasions, going before the U.S. Claims Court, U.S. District Court, and U.S. Tax Court. These were court actions that tested specific sections of the Internal Revenue Code which he found ambiguous, inequitable, and abusively interpreted by the IRS.

Disturbed by the conduct of the IRS and by the general lack of tax knowledge by most individuals, he began an innovative series of taxpayer-oriented Federal tax guides. To fulfill this need, he undertook the writing of a series of guidebooks that provide in-depth knowledge on one tax subject at a time. He focuses on subjects that plague taxpayers all throughout the year. Hence, his formulation of the "Allyear" Tax Guides. This book is one in the series. Several have already been completed (see listing on next page) and others are in process.

The author is indebted to his wife, Irma Jean, and daughter, Barbara MacRae, for the word processing and computer graphics that turn his experiences into the reality of these publications. Holmes welcomes comments, questions, and suggestions from his readers. He can be contacted in California at (408) 867-2628, or by writing to the publisher's address.

ALLYEAR Tax Guides
by Holmes F. Crouch